The Art of Getting Over Yourself

And Why You'll Be Happier When You Do

Jon Leonetti

D1530862

Life is one big exodus out of one's head and into reality; out of self-absorption (be it self-inflating or self-inflicting) and into the presence of God. Jon's latest book is an excellent roadmap to the promise land and into the joy that follows!

– **Chris Stefanick**
Founder of Real Life Catholic

Jon Leonetti has done it again. In this book, he has woven together brilliant insights from the saints, alongside his own life, to help us all become who God made us to be: saints. Inspiring. Engaging. And fun. Well done!

– **Allen Hunt**
Best-selling author and Senior Adviser at Dynamic Catholic

Feeling distant from God, spiritually stuck, or too proud to ask for the help you need to figure it all out? Turn to Jon Leonetti's *The Art of Getting Over Yourself: And Why You'll Be Happier When You Do* for a mix of approachable, real-world insights, and time-tested wisdom from the saints. This page-turner has the power to help you get over your biggest obstacle to being saintly: yourself.

– **Lisa M. Hendey**
Author of The Grace of Yes
Founder of CatholicMom.com

Few authors can capture the heart while illuminating the mind, but Jon Leonetti is absolutely one of them. A gifted storyteller and "covert" catechist, Leonetti's writing style is refreshingly approachable and engaging to all ages. *The Art of Getting Over Yourself* is a timely dagger into the heart of a modern culture obsessed with self. His candor speaks volumes while his Catholicism strikes chords. This is a solid read for every soul looking to get out of God's way—beginning with myself."

– **Mark Hart**
Catholic speaker and best-selling author

It's not about you, and it's not about me. It's about God! This book shows us the path to true joy."

– **Matt Birk**
Superbowl Champion and NFL Man of the Year

Jon Leonetti has hit it out of the park! With his delightful, conversational style, punctuated with humor and thought-provoking questions, Jon gets to the heart of what it's going to take to attain true and lasting happiness. You will not want to put this book down! The world will be a much better place if, by God's grace, each reader cultivates what is so beautifully proposed in this rich and engaging book."

– **Melissa Overmyer**
*Author of **Born to Soar***

Jon Leonetti has provided us with profound reflection on the urgency of getting over yourself. His challenging message is rooted in Christology and permeated within the truths of the Catholic faith. I have no doubt this book will change many lives!"

– Dr. Bud Marr
Director of the National Institute for Newman Studies

In a world where everybody has something to say about the "key" to happiness, Jon Leonetti breaks through all of the noise and proposes to us a game-changing truth: if you truly want to be happy, make a decision everyday to get over yourself. This powerful new book simply reminds us again about the foundational key to the Christian life—less of me and more of you. This gospel truth must become the truth of our lives, and this book is the place to start.

– Bro. Angelus Montgomery
Franciscan Friar of the Renewal

Funny, challenging, accessible, and most importantly, a blueprint for real happiness. Jon Leonetti has provided us with a much-needed antidote to our self-absorbed culture. I highly recommend it!

– Adam Storey
Director of Marriage and Family Life
for the Diocese of Des Moines

The Art of Getting Over Yourself
And Why You'll Be Happier When You Do

© 2017 by Jon Leonetti

To my mother who is humble, generous, and loving

(I have so much to learn.)

TABLE OF CONTENTS

He must increase; I must decrease.

– St. John the Baptist

INTRODUCTION

W HEN OUR LIVES stop being about *us*, when we cease being self-important and become *others-centered*, when we finally let go of all those things that hold us back: selfishness, resentment, ego, the illusion of self-sufficiency, the plans *we have* for our lives without respect to God, the mistakes we've made that we can't let go, this is when we can really start *living* and *loving* as we were always meant to do. And it's also the first and best step toward true and lasting happiness—what you've always wanted, what you've always been looking for.

CHAPTER ONE

STUCK ON YOU

*Give me a soul that knows not boredom, grumblings,
sighs, and laments, nor excess of stress, because of that
obstructing thing called "I."*

– St. Thomas More

A S HUMAN BEINGS, we have a tendency to *get stuck* on
things. Little kids, especially when first learning a new
thing, will become obsessed with it and talk about that thing,
and that thing only, for weeks on end. Remember how much
you loved dinosaurs as a kid, or dolphins, or Legos? Grown-
ups do the same thing, though for us it usually has more to
do with work, finances, relationships, or maybe whatever we're
binge-watching these days on Netflix or Hulu. Of course, there's
nothing wrong with getting stuck on things so long as they're
important, but the point is we all do get stuck, and when it happens, whether good or bad, it's hard to overcome.

People usually use the phrase "Get over yourself" sarcasti-
cally. It's a way of gently or sometimes not-so-gently pointing
out to someone that their interior compass is pointing in the
wrong direction; that they're viewing themselves as the center
of the universe—which they're not. "Get over yourself" is a
kind of shorthand for "It's not all about you," or "There are other

considerations here," or even, "C'mon, you're not *that* special." But in truth, those three little words, "Get over yourself" are packed with wit and wisdom from the Christian tradition. And as it turns out, when all is said and done, getting over ourselves is one of the main objectives of the Christian life; getting *unstuck* on ourselves.

I remember taking golf lessons as a kid. At the beginning of each lesson, my coach, who's probably still better than me in his 80s, would always demonstrate two ways of swinging the club or reading a green. The first demonstration was always "How *not* to do it," and the second was always "This is how to do it." Most golf coaches today will tell you that when teaching a new skill, it's usually best to teach someone *how to do* the thing you want them to do first, and only then point out the errors or improvements as time goes on; but coach had his system and it seemed to work (though you wouldn't know it considering my golf game today). I mention this only to help you understand how I've crafted this book. In a way, I wrote it like my childhood golf coach taught—with "how-to" and "how-*not*-to" points, as well as stories helping us attain what we all want: a more fulfilling life now and life eternal with God forever.

It's important to know right out of the gate that the point of this book is not to help you get over yourself because *you* are a problem. *You* are not the problem. The problem, or rather, *problems,* are all the things that are getting in the way of you being who you've been created to be. Getting over yourself *is not* about tearing down your sense of self or destroying a healthy sense of self-esteem. It is about getting rid of the bad ideas that hold us back, overcoming the unhelpful habits of thinking and acting that seem to get in our way, and of coming to see the world with new eyes, loving ourselves and those around us the way God does.

In short, this book is about "Saint-Making"—not the Plaster-of-Paris, stained-glass window kinds of saints you see in churches on Sunday, but the nitty, gritty, mom and dad, brother and sister, aunt and uncle, neighbor and friend sorts of saints those images represent—the great cloud of witnesses that make up the Church in heaven, and the group we long to join when we die.

THE PHRASE "GET OVER YOURSELF" IS NOT ABOUT

- **Destroying a person's sense of self-worth**
  In fact, we mean to bring it up.
- **Beating ourselves up**
  This self-contempt is always self-destructive.
- **Wallowing in our guilt**
  Guilt is a healthy response to having done something we think is wrong, but it's meant to be temporary—and to move us to action.
- **Tearing down our good qualities**
  You can't move past the place of constantly trying to improve yourself until you've come to recognize what's good about you and what you're good at.

- **Reminding us of our bad qualities**
  A healthy awareness of our weaknesses is key, but nobody ever got anywhere focusing on his weaknesses.

THE PHRASE "GET OVER YOURSELF" IS ABOUT

- **Learning to see yourself as God sees you**
- **Learning to love yourself as God loves you**
- **Learning to love others as God loves them**
- **Growing in gratitude**
- **Taking care of ourselves responsibly**
- **Taking care of others responsibly**
- **Processing the past and growing from it**
- **Learning to forgive ourselves and others**
- **Growing in trust for God and others**
- **Separating the "real me" from the "me" I make up in my head**
- **Resetting my expectations**
- **Holding myself accountable**

Getting over yourself is a worthy goal. Almost every spiritual manual in the history of the Church begins with some form of it, and all the Doctors of the Church talk about letting go of the false sense of self and growing into the "you" that you were always meant to be. The work of getting over yourself is never altogether done. If you've read any of the writings of St.

Teresa of Calcutta that were released after her death, then you know well enough that while she got over certain parts of herself very early on, others plagued her to the very end. But the *purpose* of getting over yourself is about more than checking a box on your spiritual to-do list; it's to enable you to have more freedom in your relationship with God and in your service to your brothers and sisters.

Jesus was fully divine: He was born of a virgin, worked a bunch of miracles, died and rose from the dead. He, of all people, had every reason to be stuck on Himself. But He wasn't. The Devil tried tempting Him anyway, but it didn't work. Jesus knew better. He knew where true power comes from. Ultimately, the Devil tried one of his oldest tricks—but his methods proved futile against the Son of God. And if he tried with God, you know he's trying with us. How? By getting us to worry about what people think of us for one. And how about placing our trust in anything and anyone but God? Sound familiar? These are just two of the tricks the Devil plays (repeatedly) to get us focused on ourselves. And when we focus on ourselves, we're miserable. Jesus said "No" to them; and in that moment, He showed us the posture we are to take with our lives too—a posture focused solely on God.

So many of us have a problem saying "No." And I get it. It's hard to say no to the extra piece of cake, to the magazine in the checkout line, to the extra episode on Netflix. Now more than ever we're working more hours, taking on more projects than we can handle, spending money we don't have on Christmas gifts, and maxing out our credit cards on things we don't really *need*. The problem with many of us isn't that we don't have enough. It's that we have too much. And when that happens, we blind ourselves to the One who will fulfill us: God.

Jesus, was a master at saying no. Teaching us this powerful word in the most unlikely of places, and providing us with a model to better ourselves and the people we care about most, Jesus made clear that if we're going to live a happy and healthy life, we must learn to say no and say no often. Jesus taught us this in the most unlikely of places, the desert. Jesus went out to the desert to fast and pray. The tempter knew that, of course, which is why the temptation came first in the form of bread. Jesus didn't say no because He was worried about carbs; He said no because He cared about God—He wanted his relationship with the Father to be so primary that it affected even how He ate. We're going to deal with fasting more explicitly later in this book, but it might be a good idea right now, at the very beginning, to figure out which things you can begin to cut out of your life—again, not because they're bad, but because you want to focus on what's better.

The Devil follows up by taking Jesus to the top of the Temple. Now, Jesus could rightly lay claim to all of Jerusalem—to all of the world—but that didn't stop Satan from tempting Jesus anyway. But Jesus is not concerned about what people think of

Him, at least in that way; He's not after the acclaim of others because He needs it for His own sense of self or validation. Jesus says "No" not only to Satan but also to false ideas about the self, He says "No" to depending upon others for our sense of worth and integrity, and He says "No" to all of the things that come from that: gossip, keeping up with the Joneses, making sure our kids are in all the right programs, staying hip (which I gave up on long ago), and playing into social pecking orders. He says "No" to all of it to show us that we can say "No" too.

Finally, when the Evil One takes Jesus up the mountain and commands Him to worship him, Jesus says "No"—no to false gods and no to false values. Jesus knows who is most important. Jesus knows who is God, and He's not about to let some second-rate imposter get in the way. Jesus says "No" on the mountaintop—not just to the Devil and the Darkness, but to everything that could take the place of God in our lives. Jesus has something better in mind, and He shows us how to accomplish it all the way up to the cross.

If we want to have any hope of getting over ourselves, we need to start by saying "No" to the wrong things and "Yes" to the right ones. The trick is that the wrong things are not simply those which are *obviously* wrong, but might just be wrong for me *right now*. For instance, if I have four kids under five at home and my wife and I both work, now might not be the time in my life to focus on volunteering. It doesn't mean I'll never volunteer, but if I allow myself to get caught up in something and my wife has a disproportionate burden of caring for our kids, then my love has gotten out of order, and I need to hit the reset button and *get over myself*: "Bye-bye, Mr. Perfect Volunteer." Likewise, if I have an especially needy friend, but her neediness is overwhelming my ability to keep up with my work and be present to my husband, then I might need to reset boundaries in that relationship, both in order to be a responsible adult and a good wife, but also to help my friend become less dependent—even if it means letting go of her thinking of me as the greatest friend she's ever had.

There will be more on this later, but for now, it's important for us to take some spiritual inventory if we're going to move forward. Take a few minutes to think about (or discuss) the following question:

QUESTION FOR REFLECTION

What are the things or who are the people in my life that I need to say "No" to right now, in order to make more room for God?

CHAPTER TWO

CROSSROADS

No one, however weak, is denied a share in the victory of the cross.

– St. Leo the Great

I'M GOING TO do something now that most authors would never do. I'm going to violate literally rule number one of getting people to read your book. Most writers would never admit that one chapter is more important than another, but I'm here to tell you, right here and right now, this is the most important chapter of the book. It might be the most important chapter I've ever written. So if you decide to put this book down and never pick it up again; that's fine, just finish this chapter first.

What I'm about to describe here is pretty graphic. It's a story that you already know, and you probably think you know it pretty well. The problem is that this story has been told and retold so many times and in so many different situations that it has been sanitized, whitewashed, and covered over so much that the truth of it is hard to see. I want to tell you the truth of what happened, and I want to tell it to you straight, so that there's no confusion. It won't be easy to read, and believe me, it's not easy to write, but it's important—no, it's vital—if we want to see what it takes to finally get over ourselves.

But before we begin, I want you to imagine yourself at a crossroads. You're coming up from one end, and you can either keep moving forward as you are, or turn to the right or to the left. Most of us probably do this every day, probably more times than we can count. But for our ancestors the crossroads were a mystical place, a place where different paths converged. At the crossroads one could choose to move forward or turn back, to turn left or turn right. Crossroads were symbolic of the building blocks of our lives, namely, decisions, both good and bad.

On the south side of Rome, there's a crossroads just like that. It'll take you either back into the city or out toward the country. You can turn one direction toward the sea or the other direction toward the hill country. And there's a church built right there at the crossroads. That church marks the spot where St. Peter found himself at the end of his life, having to make a decision. You see, when the persecutions got too bad and Peter was sure he was going to be killed, he tried to run away one last time. And as he came to those crossroads on the way out of the city, he saw a figure walking toward him. As the man got closer Peter recognized him: it was Jesus. Peter said to Him, "Lord, where are You going?"

And Jesus replied, "I'm going to Rome to be crucified again."

And with that reply, Peter knew which direction he had to

go, and he turned around and joined the Lord in Rome, where he too was crucified.

When Peter agreed to return to Rome he knew exactly what kind of fate awaited him. It wasn't just the friends and family he'd seen tortured and executed over the course of the last year or so. It came from the words of Jesus Himself, way back at the beginning, *"Whoever wishes to come after me must deny himself, take up his cross, and follow me"* (Matt. 16:24). We think of this automatically as a metaphorical statement, but for the disciples it was anything but a metaphor. They were *surrounded* by crucifixions.

The Romans had learned crucifixion from the Syrians, who had actually forbidden the practice as too extreme a form of torture. They had learned it from the Persians, and the Persians in turn had probably learned from somebody else. But wherever it first came from and however it was used, the purpose of crucifixion was always the same: to cause the maximum amount of pain possible to the person being crucified, and to terrify anybody else who witnessed the execution.

The crucifixes that we have hanging on our walls or chained around our necks are dainty and neat. The cross on which Jesus died was stained and bloody and smelly. We make the Sign of the Cross a dozen times a day and I, for one, seldom pause to think that I am signing myself with the first-century equivalent of a lynch rope or an electric chair.

The cross ultimately becomes the great sign of Christian hope, but it can only *become* that sign because it starts off as something much darker. Crucifixion was the punishment reserved for pirates and slaves and enemies of the state. It was for people who didn't know their place and so had to be put in it once and for all.

Whenever there was a minor uprising or a riot or some other rabble-rousing, and the trouble-causing people came to the attention of the Roman officials, they were stripped naked, beaten within an inch of their lives, and then tied or nailed to bits of wood as a warning to everyone else: "Mess with us, and THIS is what you get." When Jerusalem fell to the Romans some forty years after Jesus' death, they crucified all of the rebels by nailing them to the walls of the city—just so everyone would be perfectly clear on what was allowed and what was not.

According to the accounts given in the four gospels, Jesus' crucifixion was especially brutal. Mel Gibson tried to capture this brutality in *The Passion of the Christ* a number of years ago, and people went a little crazy. There were even stories of people vomiting in movie theatres. Now, *The Passion* might not be your favorite Jesus movie for any number of reasons, but the truth it tries to tell is important for all of us, whether or not we can bear to watch it. The crucifixion was not some pretty-as-a-picture holy card; it was brutal, gross, and cruel beyond what most of us will ever experience in our lifetimes.

Jesus was first stripped. This was routinely done before a person was flogged in order to prevent their clothes from getting in the way of the whips. He was scourged first, which was a particularly nasty method for whipping a person. The whips the Romans used had bits of stone, metal, and bone woven into the straps so that the flesh would not only bruise but would tear open. Jesus was sentenced to 39 lashes—40 was execution. Caesar wanted to go as far as he could in this punishment, without actually killing Jesus.

Then the soldiers humiliated our Lord further—first by dressing Him in the seamless gown and then by jamming the crown of thorns down onto His skull. Finally, He was paraded before the crowd who were given one more chance to bestow mercy—which they loudly rejected. Jesus would then have been strapped to the cross or at least to the piece on which His arms would eventually rest and made to march ten football fields toward the place of execution.

This walk, which we now remember whenever we pray the Stations of the Cross, was meant as a kind of last torture for the victim. The idea was that the victim was already bruised and bloody, probably weak, and now carrying a heavy burden of at least eighty pounds. Tradition tells us that Jesus fell at least three times, and if He were burdened to the cross, He wouldn't have been able to break His own fall. He would have landed on His face, the heavy burden weighing Him down and probably jamming some of the thorns into His skull or even His eyes. All the while the crowds which lined the streets—and thousands of visitors would have been in Jerusalem for the Passover—were jeering at Him and mocking Him. Eventually the exhaustion overcame Him, as it often did when the soldiers did too good a job with the scourging, and so they had to press a bystander into helping Him carry the burden up to Golgotha.

Once they arrived at the place of execution, a place already littered with the remains of past crucifixions and probably bits of bodies left behind, He was prepared to die. First, the fancy robe they had put on Him in order to make fun of Him was stripped off, ripping open the wounds on His back and starting the bleeding again. Then Jesus was pressed down upon the wood and probably first tied, then nailed to the plank. Usually the Romans left the long piece in the ground and then hoisted the person, already impaled to the wood, up onto the pole that was already set up. In any case, He was lifted up, and His hands and feet were affixed to the wood of the cross by nails.

A lot of people fuss over just where the nails were placed, but that really misses the point. It's true that if you try to nail someone to a piece of wood by the palm that the person's body weight is going to rip the nail out through the webbing of the hand, but that isn't what they were doing anyway. The crucified person was always bound with ropes to the wood, then, if the Romans wanted to make a particularly good example out of him, the person would be nailed to it as well. In either case, the person dies from the crucifixion itself; the nails simply make it a whole lot more painful. That's because when you drive a nail through a person's wrist or hand, you wind up hitting the major nerve center for the whole hand. The same thing happens with the feet. That's important for what comes next.

People who are crucified die from all sorts of causes: exhaustion, blood loss, dehydration, arrhythmia. But the most common cause of death in cases of crucifixion is asphyxiation. This seems counter-intuitive because a crucified person is forced into a position where his chest is expanded, and when the person is trying to take a deep breath, he puffs out his chest. The problem is that the person on the cross can breathe out but has trouble breathing back in, and in order to get enough leverage to breathe back in, he has to lift himself up against the wood, which is difficult when bound, but positively agonizing when he has nails driven through his hands and feet, both of which are sitting on major nerves. Eventually, the person would simply become too exhausted to press up against the pain anymore, his lungs would begin to fill with fluid, and he would suffocate to death.

We know that Jesus' crucifixion was especially brutal, at least in part, because He died so quickly. Jesus is said to have died after about six hours on the cross—from about nine in the morning to three in the afternoon. Most victims of crucifixion would linger for days. Sometimes, as an act of mercy, the soldiers would break the legs of those who were lingering, hastening their death and preventing them from pressing up against the wood to breathe. But when they came to Jesus, they saw He was already dead, and so they didn't do that; instead, a soldier pierced Him with a lance.

The water and blood, which flowed from His side, have both symbolic and biological significance. Biologically speaking, the result of all the trauma He had endured would have resulted in fluid gathering around His heart and lungs, making it progressively harder to breathe and harder for His heart to beat effectively. Spiritually speaking, this sign of blood and water, the clear and definitive sign that He was truly dead, is seen as the birth of the Church, Christ's bride, from His side; just as the woman was taken from Adam's side. The Fathers of the Church saw this as a sign of the source of the sacraments; Baptism and Eucharist are signified by the water and the blood, but what makes them effective and fruitful is the death that took place on those rough planks of wood.

It might seem strange to us that the apostles and their earliest followers saw deep spiritual significance in the reactions of Christ's body to trauma, but it seems to be the way Jesus Himself understood what was going to happen to Him and has consistently been the way the Church came to find meaning in the horror of the crucifixion. Christ's death is once and for all; it happened one day at one time in one place, and it accomplished everything it needed to. But for that death to be fruitful for us, for it to take root in our lives and change everything the way that it's supposed to, we have to participate too. And the way that Jesus calls us to participate is in His cross. I didn't make that up, and no cardinal at the Vatican sipping espresso made it up, either. Jesus said it: *"Whoever wishes to come after me must deny himself, take up his cross, and follow me"* (Matt. 16:24).

Now, I know where I'm from, when the priest or deacon is reading the Gospel at Mass, there are some who will…how should I say this?…zone out (I'm sure that never happens in your Church). Read these next few words carefully, though: *everyone heard Jesus say those words.* There was no zoning out. Why? Because they knew what the cross was, and it wasn't pretty. The word *excruciating* comes from the Latin: *ex + crucis*; it doesn't just mean "super painful." Instead, the word means literally, "out from the cross." Jesus, the One whom they were ready to follow, gave them the way to discipleship, and that way is Calvary.

Persecution was a fact of life for the earliest Christians. From the very beginning, the Church recognized those who were most perfectly united to Christ in His sufferings as martyrs—those who witnessed with their blood the faith they had in Jesus. That's because, like Him, they died, and they often died cruel and painful deaths. There isn't a more heroic way of getting over yourself than giving your life for God. And though we'd like to think this sort of thing doesn't happen anymore, we know it does. There are new martyrs everyday in the Catholic Church. And the irony, what their persecutors have never learned, is this witness of dying for Christ among Christians only strengthens His Church, which is why Tertullian, writing in A.D. 197 could write, "The blood of the martyrs is the seed of the Church."

Now, most of us reading this book probably won't suffer the kinds of death that the martyrs have and are experiencing around the world because of their faith in Jesus Christ. *Could* we suffer death because of our faith? Sure. But not likely. In the West, most of the suffering we experience for being Catholic is a late night talk show host ridiculing our Church, or a friend or family member thinking we're weird because of all the saint statues we have around our house (I embrace the weirdness). I write this because I don't want you to think you have to literally die for Jesus to live as a martyr (witness) in His Church today. There's another death that we must take on if we're going to discover the very meaning of our lives, a death which is the entire point of this book—a death to ourselves.

A lot of people get Jesus wrong in our world today. For one, many tend to think of Jesus as *nice*. He didn't ruffle any feathers, and He gave everyone a fuzzy feeling inside. Those who think like this obviously aren't reading the same Gospel I'm reading. Jesus was anything but *nice*. *Nice* is a virtue of the world and normally applies to a person who doesn't make waves. Jesus made waves. Lots of waves. He flipped tables and yelled at people too, and He most certainly didn't make people comfortable. That's why they killed Him. It's the only thing they thought they could do with Him. They certainly didn't ignore Him, and no one was indifferent to Him. (You don't hang people on trees to whom you're indifferent.) This is why indifferentism to the faith is worse than hatred. I can have a conversation with someone who hates our faith (believe me, I've had many), but those who don't care or who are indifferent to Catholicism have already left the conversation, and frankly, are the hardest to get back.

Jesus turned everything the people of His day thought upside-down. He made clear: the system isn't working the way it should, and it needs to be destroyed. What system? The system that parades selfishness, pride, ego, greed, resentment, looking out for number one, and evening the score as the way our lives should be lived. It didn't work then, and it certainly doesn't work now. And they, like many today, hated Him for it. But Jesus was right. And it doesn't take a sociologist to figure it out. Think about it. Why is there such a happiness crisis in our world today? Because our sports teams aren't winning? No. Because we've chosen ourselves over God.

We've replaced selflessness with selfishness and forgiveness with resentment. We've turned in on ourselves. This is why the cross is so vital—and why we hang them in every Catholic Church around the world and place them on the walls of our homes. The cross represents the life you and I have always been longing to live. It's why St. Paul said that he preached the crucified Lord (1 Corinthians 1:23) and why every saint you've ever heard of embraced the cross as his or her primary way of life. Is it easy? Of course not! But what in life that's worth it is easy? Getting over ourselves is never easy, and it certainly doesn't always feel good. This is why St. Teresa of Calcutta would continually point to the cross and remind her sisters that love hurts. Loving and forgiving your enemy hurts (ask anyone who has an enemy). But it's necessary in order to live the life Jesus is calling us to live. It's necessary if you want to be happy in this life and in the next.

QUESTION FOR REFLECTION

What or who in my life is getting in the way of a right relationship with God?

CHAPTER THREE

THE GOOD, THE BAD, AND THE WORLD'S WORST SIN

Do you wish to rise? Begin by descending.

– St. Augustine

SAINT AUGUSTINE IS probably best remembered today for his struggles with lust. Most people would say that was his greatest sin. After all, he was a fourth-century playboy who had his pick of the women of the day, who managed to father a child with his live-in girlfriend before converting to Catholicism and, in the midst of his conversion, spouts one of the more famous (and hilarious) prayers in Christian history: "Give me chastity, O Lord, *but not yet!*"

Yes, Augustine's struggle with lust was very real, and through a lot of prayer and sacrifice he was victorious, but the answer to Augustine's prayer didn't come by figuring out the perfect strategy to do away with sexual temptation, or how to avoid occasions of sin, or even by disciplining his body (though he tried all of these a lot). Instead, Augustine was only able to overcome *lust* when he realized that this was the symptom, rather than the cause of his disordered life. That cause that he identified in himself, and so in all of us, was *pride*.

What's ironic about this is that of all the people who ever lived, Saint Augustine had every reason to be proud. Even if he'd never become a Christian and one of the most influential theologians in Church history, he would undoubtedly be remembered as one of the greatest orators of all time and probably would have gone on to serve in some official capacity in the Roman Empire. He was, simply, one of the brightest, best, and most fortunate men of his generation.

By the age of thirty, he held one of the most prominent academic posts in the whole of the Roman Empire. His girlfriend was known as one of the most beautiful women around, and he was a star in his cult. *Manicheanism* was a kind of pseudo-religious group that everyone who was anyone dabbled in at least a little; it emphasized spirituality over religious practice, had a complicated mythology that you were only let in on bit by bit, and was fundamentally dualistic—the material world was bad and the creation of an evil god, and the spiritual world was good and the creation of a good god. This made it an incredibly convenient belief system for those who were not convinced about the old pagan gods but were unwilling to conform to the stricter morality of their Christian neighbors.

Augustine was no stranger to the Church, however. His father was a non-practicing pagan, but his mother was a devout Catholic who had been trying to get him to convert more or less since he'd taken up with his mistress, at around eighteen.

When Augustine finally settled in Milan, his mother actually moved in with him and kept pressing him to come to church with her to hear the bishop preach. That preacher, now known as St. Ambrose, taught Augustine humility, and that humility led not only to the chastity he was afraid to ask for, but to the conversion he didn't even know he needed.

Ambrose, the bishop of Milan, was himself a famous convert. He had been a kind of Augustine-type character just a generation before, and in fact had been a major government official when he was elected bishop. At first Augustine just went to hear him preach, because he was a speech professor and he wanted to see what the older man's techniques were all about. And Ambrose was good—one of the best he'd ever seen—but Augustine had so long ago decided that Christianity was silly; he wasn't even really paying attention to the older man's arguments. Even still, a kind of friendship grew between them, fostering many deep and meaningful conversations about life and God.

Slowly, over time, without even realizing it was happening, Augustine began to see the truth of what Ambrose was saying. But this was terrible news for Augustine, since he'd long ago decided that Christianity wasn't true. In the end, it took a providential and serendipitous event to show Augustine he wasn't altogether in charge of his life. He had just had a fight with his best friend, Alypius, and walked out into the courtyard to calm himself down. He was, by this point, basically convinced of the *truth* of the Catholic Church, but he was very much afraid to enter, because he knew that his moral life was a wreck. He sat down on a bench to cry, and while he was weeping heard the voice of children, probably from the neighbor's yard, chanting, *"Tolle, legge!"* or, "Take and read!" Part of what he and his buddy had been arguing about was Saint Antony of Egypt, who had blundered into Church one day just as they were chanting the passage from St. Matthew, *"If you wish to be perfect, go, sell what you have and give to [the] poor, and you will have treasure in heaven. Then come, follow me."* (Matt 19:21) He interpreted the children's playground chant to be an invitation to do the same, so he returned to the house and opened the copy of the scriptures which he had. This little game of "Bible Roulette" landed on the line from St. Paul, *"Let us conduct ourselves properly as in the day, not in orgies and drunkenness, not in promiscuity and licentiousness, not in rivalry and jealousy. But put on the Lord Jesus Christ, and make no provision for the desires of the flesh"* (Romans 13:13, 14).

That's all it took. He separated from his mistress and took custody of their son, and together the two of them were baptized at the next Easter Vigil. But it took an enormous amount of humility for Augustine to admit that his mother had been right all along and that he had more or less wasted twenty years of his life, following false dreams and buying wholesale into bad ideas. The brightest kid in the class still had much to learn, and the most successful man alive had to become acquainted with failure.

Once his conversion was complete and Augustine was well

and faithfully committed to his new way of life, he would write this about his transition from pride to humility:

> In my pride I was running adrift, at the mercy of every wind. You were guiding me as a helmsman steers a ship, but the course you steered was beyond my understanding. I know now, and confess it as the truth, that I admired Hierius [one of his teachers] more because others praised him than for the accomplishments for which they praised him. (*Confessions* IV.14.4)

Now I don't know about you, but when I'm tempted to buy the newest thing that pops up on my Amazon recs, or when I start supporting a new political candidate or start a different exercise regimen, *pride* is about the furthest thing from my mind. But I think what Saint Augustine is trying to teach us here is that when we get caught up in ourselves, when we get wedded to our own ideas of success or too fixed on our plans for our lives or the world, when we genuinely believe that we and we alone are the commanders of our own destiny, then we have given in to pride, and in the worst way. First, prideful people can't help but believe that everyone who has anything bad happen to them has done something to deserve it, and, in so doing, that they misdirected their own destiny. More seriously, in their state of ingratitude, prideful persons place themselves in resistance to the divine will, because they do not leave room for *God* to do what God means to do, in our lives and in our world.

I have a confession to make: whenever some of my religious or churchy friends (it's okay; I'm religious and churchy too) start to talk about "pride," my ears begin to twitch. I can't decide if it's because I think we mean different things by the word or if they just seem to overemphasize it, but my own experience of reading Augustine and what the Church's tradition identifies as the worst of sins simply doesn't match up.

As a kid, I remember craving hearing my dad say, "I'm proud of you, son." I remember that feeling that would swell up in my chest whenever I hit a ball or made a basket, which frankly didn't happen very often, and I remember being *proud* of myself. As I grew and I figured out which things I was good at and which things I wasn't, I remember being *proud* when I was able to accomplish something I didn't think I'd be able to and proud also when I did something I generally do well.

Now that I have kids I find myself proud of them, like my father was of me. I'm proud when I see them take their first steps, or finish a difficult puzzle. I make note of this because this kind of pride is *not* what the Church means by *the sin of pride*. But it's also not as simple as cockiness or arrogance; pride doesn't equal confidence plus being a jerk. Instead, pride is ultimately about truth and about justice—believing untrue things about God, ourselves, and the world, and then acting in unjust ways because of those wrong ideas. In other words, we can't get over ourselves until we really understand the kind of pride that's really hurting us and that the Lord Himself wants us to conquer.

Different saints, doctors of the Church, and other smart people in the Church's tradition have talked about pride in different ways. Probably the easiest way to break it down, however, came from a saint ironically called Gregory the Great.

VANITY

This is more than just an obsession with one's appearance, though that's often a symptom. Vanity is an easy mistake to make when it comes to pride because it happens when we recognize something good in our lives: our looks, our abilities, our talents, our financial situation, our career, our kids, or whatever, and then in looking at the good things that we have, we presume that it comes from ourselves. Now it's certainly true that most of us have worked for the things that we have obtained, but make no mistake: if you really believe that you deserve to have everything you've got and that everybody else has exactly what they deserve, then you've radically misunderstood what it means to be God and what it means to be you.

ENTITLEMENT

We talk about entitlement a lot in our society, especially in terms of certain groups of people feeling "entitled" to particular goods or services. We say that our children are *entitled* when they act like demanding brats, or call our spouse *entitled* when we're in an argument, but I don't know if we really understand the root of *entitlement*. The theological definition of *entitlement* basically means that "a person recognizes that whatever good he has obtained has come from God (either directly or through somebody else), but the person believes that he has been given the good because he deserves it." So teachers complain that children feel entitled to an "A" in class and are rightly upset when the kids don't want to work for it. A person suffering from the sin of entitlement recognizes that the money he has comes from his family, but he thinks he deserves it because his family is better than other families. This thinking leads to an attitude toward the world which expects things to happen the way a person wants them to simply because he wants it—which is, obviously, not the way things really work.

ARROGANCE

We've all known arrogant people, and they're very hard to be around—not simply because they're proud of what they have and are but because they assume, brag about, and claim things to which they aren't or don't have a right. The arrogant person *arrogates*, literally "claims for one's self" something that isn't his. It's basically what happens in the parking lot when someone cuts in front of you and takes your parking space, presuming you won't do anything about it (not that that's *ever* happened to me before). Arrogance is a particularly nasty kind of pride because it ultimately leads to some kind of theft, either in the arrogant person's head or in real life, as he *steals* a good thing (even if it's just credit or respect) that rightly belongs to someone else.

POSSESSIVENESS

Relationships are the obvious example here: the possessive boyfriend who gets jealous whenever his girl is hanging out with other guys, or the clingy, needy girlfriend who needs to hang on her boyfriend in front of other people just to make clear "he's mine." But this doesn't only happen in romantic relationships. This last kind of pride leads us to the most destructive behavior relative to other people; it wants to be the sole possessor of whatever the good thing is, that it will do everything it can to make sure that nobody else can share it. This is why athletes sabotage their competition; it's what leads to corporate and political corruption, and more often than not wriggles its way into our families and homes (think Mom and Dad's inheritance), causing the kind of division and strife that can last for years.

By his own account, Saint Augustine suffered at different times and in various ways from each form of pride. In the end, however, he found that the first and best remedy for pride was simply **gratitude**. It's hard to be proud when you're busy being grateful. Gratitude to God helps to hit the reset button on our often warped perspectives.

Probably the most warped perspective that many of us have

concerns the most important relationship in our lives—namely, God. Most of us treat God as an optional add-on, a kind of fix-it utility when everything else fails. We "say our prayers" and go to Mass on Sundays, but we often only really pray, only *really talk to God*, only *really* make any kind of attempt at a real relationship when something goes wrong. We use prayer as a last resort when it ought to be our first line of attack.

If God is God, that is, if God is everything that we say He is—everything *He's told us He is*—then He's not some sort of celestial appendage; He's what's responsible for keeping the whole thing running. This is really, really important when it comes to the question of pride. If God precedes us, that is, if He comes in time before us and if He's responsible for bringing each of us into being, then by definition, we can't merit or "earn" our own existence. The fact that we exist is a gift, pure and simple, mediated by our human parents, but granted ultimately by God. That means that the first response which the creature—that's us—owes to God *in justice* (meaning it's not just a nice thing to do, but rather to fail to do so would be wrong), is *thanksgiving*. Our most fundamental relationship to God is one of thanks; first, for the gift of life, and then for everything which we've received subsequently.

Now it's true, the gift of life is mediated by our parents. But even here, God's hand can show us something about thanksgiving. When your parents conceived you, there were more than a hundred million other possibilities that could have become you, but the *you* that *we* got is the *you* that *you are*. God doesn't choose things generically; He selects them specifically. When we give thanks to God for the gift of life, it can't be generic; it's got to be gratitude for the specific life which is mine. That's why self-hatred is so antithetical to the Christian tradition and why "getting over yourself" does not and cannot mean throwing away the gift that God has given—both to you and to us.

Because thanksgiving is so central to the creature's relationship with God, the most natural way for the Church to respond to God in faith is with the Eucharist—the Great Thanksgiving. As Americans, we celebrate Thanksgiving once a year; as Catholics we celebrate Thanksgiving every single day. Every time you go to Mass, every time the Church gathers for Mass even without you, she's giving thanks for you and for the gifts that you have received. And we, in our response to God, can only offer back that which we've already been given, both as a thanks-offering and a pledge of what's to come.

Saint Ambrose frequently reiterated to Augustine that, "There is no more urgent need in life than the duty of thanksgiving." It shouldn't surprise us, then, that Augustine's words of gratitude were similarly profound and yet deeply rooted in his own individual experience.

> People travel to wonder at the height of mountains, at the huge waves of the sea, at the long courses of rivers, at the vast compass of the ocean, at the circular motion of the stars; and they pass by themselves without wondering... Now, let us acknowledge the wonder of

our physical incarnation— that we are here, in these particular bodies, at this particular time, in these particular circumstances. May we never take for granted the gift of our individuality. (*Confessions*, 10, 35)

QUESTIONS FOR REFLECTION

Which of the four types of pride do I struggle with? How can I overcome it?

How am I doing with gratitude? What am I most grateful for? What should I be more grateful for that I often forget or neglect?

CHAPTER FOUR

THREE SAINTS WHO (ALMOST) GOT OVER THEMSELVES AND YOU CAN TOO!

Let us become saints so that after having been together on earth, we may be together in Heaven.

– St. Pio

AT THIS POINT, you could pretty easily be saying to yourself, "Okay, so becoming more aware of the role of sacrifice in my life is obviously a good thing, and certainly my spouse, my kids, my wider extended family and my friends can help me to grow in virtue, but so what? Pretty much everybody does that, and it seems like pretty much everybody dies imperfect. Is this all even really worth it?"

The question is a good one. Everyone, even the greatest of saints, struggled with sin to the very end, and the growth that we have in getting over ourselves comes so slowly that many days it doesn't seem worth it. But it is, both for the people that you know and for many that you don't. Because we see the growth in those around us incrementally, just as we see it in ourselves, we don't notice *just how much* Dad has grown since when we were little kids, and we didn't even know him before we were born. We have no idea how much better Mom is now than before she met Dad. It's like a famous interview that the novelist Evelyn Waugh gave to a journalist after his conversion to Catholicism. Waugh was notoriously sarcastic and rude, and his demeanor did not seem to change a whole lot after his conversion. When a reporter finally worked up the courage to ask him about it, he grew very serious and replied, "My dear, you have no idea how awful I would be *if I weren't a Catholic.*" In other words, "If you think I'm bad now, imagine if...."

So in order to remind ourselves why getting over ourselves really is worth it and to get just a little clearer sense of how this might work out in our lives, we need to look more closely at how it worked itself out in the lives of those who clearly were successful. We need to study the success stories and implement the life lessons of those who really did conquer pride, or at least came as close to conquering it as anyone this side of heaven. We need to return to the lives of the saints, and relying on their help and example, learn from them the lessons their humility can teach us.

I have already mentioned how St. Augustine is one of the best examples of humility in the entire history of the Church. It's rare for a person to have as much reason as Augustine did to be prideful. Nevertheless, despite having so much talent and accomplishing so much, by the end of his life Augustine

managed a humility that would be envied for ages. Two piec-
es of St. Augustine's story, which I believe were at the heart of
his success, aren't often addressed. One was his experience of
religious community, and the other was his friendship with
St. Jerome.

Augustine converted at 31 and after a year decided to return from Milan, where he had been living and working, to
North Africa, where he had been raised. His mother, St. Moni-
ca, who had been so instrumental in his conversion, died while
they were preparing for the voyage. Just a few months after
arriving home St. Augustine's own son, Adeodatus, also died.
Augustine got rid of everything except the family home itself
and turned it into a religious community.

Today, St. Augustine is thought of as a bishop, but he lived
very differently than most bishops today. He remained in the
community for his whole life and so lived not only the regular pattern of daily prayer, but shared space, things, and time
with other people—other people he might not have chosen
to live with "in the world." But far from holding him back,
Augustine saw this as an opportunity, "for the rich to grow
poor, and the poor to grow rich"—not in wealth, but in virtue.
He understood that for the rich to live more simply than they
were accustomed gave them a spiritual edge, and that for the
poor, no longer unsure of where the next meal would come
from, they could focus more intently on the things of heaven.
It was mostly the fact of living with other people that, over
the long haul, helped develop St. Augustine into the man he

would become—the man history remembers. And the insights drawn from that common life live on in the Church today in the *Rule of St. Augustine,* the guidelines for religious life that he drew up for the community which his sister wound up leading.

Today not only do the Augustinians follow this rule, but the Dominicans, the Norbertines, the Trinitarians, the Victorines, the Paulines, and most communities of Canons Regular do as well. As with everything about St. Augustine, however, the point is not that a book he wrote 1500 years ago is still being read, but that it's still worth reading; it's not that his vocation made him more humble then, but that our vocations can make us more humble right now.

Another major factor in St. Augustine's growth in humility and holiness was his relationship with St. Jerome. Now on the surface, these guys were as different as could be: Augustine the wealthy playboy turned pious Bishop; Jerome the quiet scholar who, even after his conversion to Christianity, stayed the quiet scholar. Augustine was clearly a major extrovert; he loved people and was successful as a bishop largely because of his skillful rhetoric and ability to persuade. Jerome was cold and severe, brash at all of the wrong times and silent when he should have spoken. He had to be ordained more or less by force and preferred the quiet of a cell in the desert to the hubbub of everyday life in the city and the parish. He was older than Augustine, both chronologically and in terms of his Christian conversion, so that he was already writing commentaries on Scripture while Augustine was still out carousing around Italy and figuring out whether or not God really existed. You can imagine, then, when Augustine came on the scene and started writing letters to Jerome attacking the quality of his scholarship that the senior priest was not very impressed.

Augustine enjoyed disputing with people in public, and while what drove him was always a deep commitment to the truth, he clearly took great delight in the back and forth of a good argument. Jerome did not. He was acerbic, dismissive, defensive, and sometimes downright mean. But as time wore on, it became clear that he could not simply ignore the new bishop of Hippo, and so slowly, bit-by-bit, the tone of his letters changed, and while Augustine and Jerome never came to an agreement on any number of things, they did come to have a genuine respect and love for each other.

This was as true for Augustine as it was for Jerome. Most of the people Augustine argued with in public were heretics, people who were already clearly outside the Church. Jerome, on the other hand, was one of the most highly regarded scholars in the Church and considered a living saint by any number of people. Learning to live with Jerome's impatience was good for Augustine, and growing in appreciation for Augustine and his differences was good for Jerome. Though they never met in person, together they helped each other to get over themselves, and get on to the true business of the Christian life—loving Christ and each other.

In the history of the Church, two saints have been assigned the title "patron of the impossible," or "impossible cases." These are St. Jude the apostle and St. Rita of Cascia. St. Jude's association with the impossible comes mostly from his name. One of the oldest prayers to St. Jude begins, "the name of the traitor has caused you to be forgotten by many..." *Jude* and *Judas* are the same name; different versions of their name in English are used so that the two men can be told apart.

Because he shares a name with Judas Iscariot, he has often gone forgotten, just as those in desperate situations can feel forgotten by God. St. Rita's association with the impossible, however, really reflects the impossible circumstances of her life and the way in which, over time, she overcame most of what holds back you and me.

Practically speaking, St. Rita lived two very full lives; the first as a wife and mother, and the second as a diplomat and a nun. Rita was born in 1381 in a village called Roccoporena, near Cascia in the Umbrian Mountains of central Italy. Her parents were benefactors of the Augustinian nuns who lived nearby, and as a girl, Rita talked of entering but eventually changed her mind as her parents arranged a seemingly suitable marriage for her. Unfortunately, not all was as it seemed.

Paolo Mancini was a local nobleman, very rich, and also known for his generosity to the Church and to the poor. Unfortunately, less known, at least to Rita's parents, was his quick temper, love of women, and commitment to holding a grudge. They conceived shortly after getting married, and Rita gave birth to twins, but before long, she was enduring regular physical and emotional abuse at the hands of her husband, as well as dealing with his long absences, bad financial decisions, and frequent infidelities. She raised her two sons, Giovanni and Paolo, to be fervent in the faith as she was, but their father's influence eventually won out.

Rita's husband was involved in a blood feud between his own family, the Mancinis, and another local family, the Chiqui. This feud consumed most of the couple's life and fortune, but slowly, over time, Rita was able to win her husband over to see the futility of the fight. Eventually he renounced his part in the feud and attempted to broker a peace but was betrayed by members of the Chiqui and violently murdered.

Rita gave a public pardon to her husband's murderers and ordered her sons not to take revenge. Giovanni and Paolo, however, took after their father's side of the family more than their mother's. They actively plotted revenge with the help of an uncle but died before they could carry it out. Rita, though now left childless and a widow, was grateful; at least her sons had died before becoming murderers.

Now at this point, most of us would probably have given up on life. Rita was a widow, and the Chiqui had no particular problem with her. She could have retired young and simply enjoyed what was left of the money she had inherited. But the dreams of her early life returned to her, and she decided to enter the convent at Cascia. Only this time she was refused, not by her parents, but by the nuns themselves. They were worried, not only about the scandal of having Rita enter the convent following her husband's assassination, but for the safety of the monastery itself so long as the *vendetta* remained between the two most powerful families in the area. So they made a deal with her: if she could reconcile her former in-laws and their sworn enemies, then she'd be granted a shot at religious life.

Rita's parents were kind-hearted and generous people, and so had earned the nickname *Conciliatore di Cristo* or *The Peacemakers of Christ*; Rita would follow in their footsteps. Before even approaching either family, Rita first stormed heaven with her prayers. After a suitable period of fasting and prayer she met first with her husband's family and then with their opponents. Both sides were taken aback at the young widow's courage and grace, but a lasting peace seemed impossible.

Then a near-tragedy struck; her former brother-in-law, Bernardo, contracted the bubonic plague. It looked as though he would die, and the feud would pass on to another generation, making it impossible for Rita to enter the convent. Now Rita's prayers turned to healing for Bernardo. And through her intercession, not only was Bernardo's body restored, but his heart was as well. He agreed to call off the feud, and the opposing family, moved and frankly startled by the seemingly supernatural turn of events, agreed. They signed a public treaty of reconciliation and embraced, and a fresco of this scene still stands in the Church of St. Francis at Cascia, the widow Rita hiding in the background not yet a saint, but already a peacemaker.

Rita had kept up her part of the bargain, and now the sisters did too. Rita was admitted to the community and began her religious life at thirty-six years old. She lived there for another lifetime (the next forty years), and most of it was not very interesting, at least to outsiders: prayer, fasting, penances, manual labor, cooking, cleaning, and assisting visitors to the convent. Twenty-five years after entering, however, she did have a profound experience which marked her for the rest of her life—in more ways than one.

She was praying before her favorite image, *The Jesus of Holy Saturday*, when she was deeply moved by an awareness of Christ's suffering and of His love for her and for all people. In that moment of awareness, she asked God to unite her with Jesus' suffering by sharing some small part of His pain, and she was granted an extraordinary grace. She received the holy *stigmata*—the mark of Christ—but unlike many of the others who had received wounds in their hands and feet and side, Rita received exactly what she'd asked for—a small taste of His suffering. She was given a single wound on her forehead, open and deep for the rest of her life—a single thorn from Christ's own crown.

A story is told about Rita's death that says something important about her character. The hired man who worked for the sisters and prepared Rita's coffin had been paralyzed by a stroke. The casket, therefore, was unusually simple, even for a nun, and so he was embarrassed as he presented it to the sisters to lay out Sr. Rita's body. He told them that if he were well then, he would prepare something more suitable for the holy sister, and it was at that moment that Rita worked her first miracle. The man was healed immediately and did end up making a more elaborate coffin, but Rita was never buried in it. To observers, it became clear that Rita's body was not decomposing, and so she now lies in a glass-enclosed casket there at the basilica in Cascia—an impossible end to a seemingly impossible life.

Now when you first look at it, St. Rita's story can seem so unlike our own that any comparison just seems silly. Most of us only ever live out one vocation: *either* marriage *or* religious life, not both. Plus, she married into money, and most of us have to struggle at least a little simply to get by. And while all families have problems, probably none of us have lost a spouse or children to a centuries-long family feud. But of course, that's only *part* of the story.

She was a victim of domestic violence, and like a lot of people today, didn't have or didn't know about the resources available to her to either get away or get help. She was frequently cheated on, and like many women today whose husbands are unfaithful or husbands whose wives have problems with fidelity, she simply didn't know what to do about it. The way her husband died might have been exceptional, but plenty of people lose their spouses unexpectedly, and like most of those, she really didn't know how to relate to her former in-laws afterward. She also lost her kids far too young, within a year or so of losing her husband, and so like most of us, had more than her fair share of suffering. And when she needed the Church the most, they asked her to do something she didn't think she'd be able to manage in reconciling the two families. Rita had every excuse to throw aside her faith and leave. But Rita's faith was never about her. Rita's faith was always about Christ.

It seems to me that the real lesson from St. Rita in terms of getting over yourself is precisely this: *you and you alone are not responsible for fixing everything in your life.* You have to rely on other people—both living and dead—and trust that God knows better what you're capable of than you do yourself.

Put Rita's story in contemporary terms: a girl gets married right out of high school to a rich kid who's just finishing college. His family has money, but they're in a constant struggle with the only major competitor for their business. There's always a hint of organized crime or drugs or something, and then, when the kids are older, the husband goes and gets himself killed. The boys want revenge and are planning on taking on the rival gang, but instead, they contract a weird disease and die. And then, when the young woman finally figures out what she wants to do with her life, she has to broker a truce between the two competing families.

This story is like *The Godfather* meets *A Nun's Story*; it seems too crazy to have happened, but it did, and Rita turned out better for it. But in order to do it, she *had* to rely on other people. She had to trust that her patron saints would see her through. She had to believe that the families could eventually be reconciled. And she had to believe, deep down in her bones, that if God wanted her to enter that convent that He would make it possible—even if it meant doing the impossible first.

QUESTIONS FOR REFLECTION

With which of these three saints do you most identify? Why?

How can you imitate the virtues of these saints in your own life? How can their example help you to overcome pride?

CHAPTER FIVE

HOMEWARD BOUND

If you want to bring happiness to the whole world, go home and love your family.

– St. Teresa of Calcutta

"*F*OR WHERE YOUR *treasure is, there also will your heart be*" (Matt. 6:21). Where do you put the most time and energy in your life right now? That's where your priorities are, and if you feel your priorities are somewhere else, then you're probably frustrated at having to put that much time and energy into something that you really don't want to. What we're going to try and do is get you to put your time, energy, and resources *where your heart actually is,* so that you can *get over yourself* and *get onto the business of living* a truly fulfilling life.

For most of us, those who know us best are those closest to us: our spouses, kids, parents, and close friends. Sometimes, for a variety of reasons, it happens that those who know us best are other people, but for the most part, those who are closest to us know us best, and those who know us best are the most valuable resources we have in the struggle to get over ourselves.

Those who truly know and love us know our strengths and weaknesses. They know what makes us tick. They know how to challenge us so that we'll listen, and how to challenge us in a way that will set us off. They know how to push our buttons and how to set us straight. They know what we care about most and what we think about least. And they know how to get us to change, however little, because they've seen it in us before and they believe in us.

This is why our home, whether that's a house or an apartment, a mansion or a hovel, is the best place to start trying to get over ourselves. The thing is, though, it's not only going to require a lot of work, but also a lot of trust. Because it's going to mean asking those who know you about their honest opinions of you, and you have to be willing to take that feedback—even if it hurts.

So as you begin this process of trying to get over yourself, redouble your commitments to those people in your life you care about the most. Make sure you love them more intentionally than you do when on autopilot, and make an extra effort to be there for them, to be there with them, and to be as open, honest, and caring with them as you are asking them to be with you.

We all have blind spots when it comes to ourselves. We all have ways of being in the world that are less than helpful, but we're so accustomed to being that way that we don't realize just how we're being perceived, or sometimes what we're missing. It's just like in traffic; some blind spots are there because of the way the car is built, but others appear or get worse when we're stressed, distracted by the kids in the back seat, annoyed with our spouse in the front seat, or just plain angry at ourselves for being late to whatever it is that we're driving to. And just like in the car, sometimes that spouse in the seat next to us, or even the kid in the car seat in the back, is the best equipped to say, "Hey, Dad, can you see that semi coming up along the left?" The trick is to listen without blaming and not to worry about who is right and who is wrong. We must have the humility to take correction from someone else—even if later on we might have to correct that same person ourselves.

The nature-nurture debate is as old as the hills, and while we can still argue the specifics, the bottom line is this: certain features of our personality—the way we think, feel, act, and interact with the world—are inbuilt. They're unconscious predispositions, and because they're unconscious and because we live with them for most or all of our lives, we often don't notice them as much as other people do. For instance, I've known since I was a kid that I chew my nails. My parents made a few attempts to stop me in grade school, and it would get better or worse year to year and in times of stress or lack of stress. It wasn't until I met my wife and she started to really get to know me and to really help me stop chewing my nails that I came to realize just how much I chewed them. Now, chewing your nails might be a little bit gross, but it's not normally a super-destructive habit. Not all of our inclinations and dispositions are so neutral, however.

Genetic science today tells us that people are born with predispositions to everything from alcoholism to breast cancer to musical ability. Of course, these predispositions usually aren't automatic; you can't *become* an alcoholic unless you start to drink—no matter what your genes are. You'll never become a virtuoso if you're never given an instrument to play. Likewise, our life experiences shape our expectations and our ability to develop our talents. If our parents, teachers, and other responsible adults constantly tell us we'll never be any good at anything, it's going to be very, very difficult to work against all of that and become just a functional adult, let alone a success.

Most of us spend a good part of our lives trying to name and claim our good dispositions, to grow them and develop them and succeed with them, as well as minimize our bad inclinations, so that we get in as little trouble as we can. We practice our sport if we're good at it and keep going to the gym long after we've quit competing. We avoid spicy foods if they give us gas, or sweets if we have a hard time with weight. It turns out that our moral lives aren't so different. Most of us tend, as naturally as we do with sports and music, to particular virtues and particular vices. Of course, some people have more talent than others, and other people more health problems, and so some people tend to more than one virtue, and others to more than one vice. But, generally speaking, most of us have a kind of preference—again, either inbuilt or learned—for one or two good things and one or two bad things. And as it happens, the best way to combat our dominant vices is usually with our dominant virtues.

As a rule, most people who struggle with lust don't also struggle with greed. Their mind and heart are too occupied with satisfying their sexual desire to have time to focus on acquiring stuff. Likewise, a person who tends to gossip doesn't also tend to theft. Now that's not to say that no burglar has ever gossiped about somebody or no person who has struggled with lust has ever stolen something, but in terms of our *dominant* dispositions—those that take up most of our time and energy—well, most of us only have enough time and energy for one or two. If they do bleed over, they tend to go together.

So if I struggle with lust, which is basically not being able to say "No" to my sexual desires, then I might also struggle with saying "No" to myself with food or drink. Likewise, if I tend to be greedy in terms of money, I probably am also greedy when it comes to power, or friends, or relationships. The trick is learning to know ourselves from the inside out so that we can recognize our own tendencies to our own particular sort of badness and so head it off at the pass.

Let's imagine it this way. Katie is a thirty-two-year-old wife and mother of two. She teaches science at the local public high school and is an active member of her parish, serving on the RCIA team and helping to coordinate the annual fundraising gala. She has many gifts: she's an excellent public speaker (hence the RCIA work), a top-notch organizer (why the gala goes so smoothly), and has a good mind for detail (which is what makes her such an effective science teacher).

Unfortunately, Katie's greatest gifts also play into her greatest weaknesses. She is a terrible gossip, and her work with both the gala and RCIA puts her into contact with some very privileged information. She knows, for instance, that one of the people in RCIA is not going to be received into the Church at Easter because he's waiting on an annulment. That's pretty privileged information, but when a neighbor tells the story of somebody else in the same situation, she can't help but share what she knows. Likewise, with the gala, while the other committee members are happy that she's there to help coordinate the event, they don't want her to have access to the financial records because they're afraid she'll start telling people how much other people are donating.

Katie can't see her problem; her friends and fellow-parishioners can, but they are afraid to approach her about it. Her husband, however, is able both to challenge her tendency toward gossip but also encourage her tight-as-a-drum memory. She starts to memorize things as "confidential" or "not confidential" and so is able to avoid the tendency to share information she shouldn't.

On the face of it, Katie has a natural tendency toward gossip and lack of self-control, and she learns to overcome it through her relationship with her husband. And that seems like a perfectly *natural* thing to do; but it's really *supernatural*. Why? Because the relationship between husband and wife has been ordained by God, and in the case of Christians, is itself a *sacrament*—a means of a particular grace—so that part of the reason Katie is married to her husband is precisely for *him* to help her overcome her vices.

Now it's true; most of us who are married often experience this as much as growing to tolerate our spouse's weaknesses, and growth in patience on both sides is certainly part and parcel of what marriage is all about. But no spouse should ever be content with their partner's vices. We aren't called to nag each other all of the time, but we are called to challenge one another to become holy. If your husband has a tendency to drink too much, then you have an obligation *to him* as well as to yourself to challenge him on it (provided it's safe to do so; if it's not, you probably have an obligation to get out of the situation and get professional help for the both of you). Likewise, if your wife has a tendency to talk down to you, then you need to call her on it—not because it hurts your feelings when she's mean to you or the kids, but because *it's bad for her* to be that way. The Fathers at Vatican II wrote that "This grace proper to the sacrament of Matrimony is intended to perfect the couple's love and to strengthen their indissoluble unity" (*Lumen Gentium*, 11).

Perfect the couple's love and strengthen their indissoluble unity. That might sound kind of overwhelming, but it's really just a fancy way of saying, "Help each other get over themselves." That in the end is what Christian marriage is all about, and it's why marriage is called a "school of charity." Quite simply, marriage is one of the best and most effective means of getting over yourself ever imagined.

If you're married, you're probably already laughing and shaking your head in agreement. Marriage has a way of humbling us, calling us out of ourselves in total abandonment, which is precisely what love is supposed to do. People often ask me why my first book, *Mission of the Family*, was on the family. Why did I choose to start there? Heck, I had just gotten married, and we hadn't even had our first kid yet. But the reason that I chose to start there was because even then I knew that the family is where it all starts. It's why Teresa and I chose to get married in the first place!

Even if you're not married now with a family, you most likely grew up in one, so you know what I mean. Even if your family wasn't perfect (mine wasn't either, by a long shot), you had to learn to get over yourself, and if you were going to start doing that as a kid, it was only going to be possible if your parents were at least trying to do so as well—no matter how imperfect they might be.

I'll never forget our wedding day. It was as magical as the movies make out and maybe even more so. Three hundred people gathered in the church, my wife looked stunning walking down the aisle, and for the first time anybody could remember, I was speechless. I'm grateful for the memories of the day and that we could start our marriage off on such a high note, but anybody who has been married for more than about three minutes knows that doesn't last. Sure, there are some exceptionally beautiful moments: birthdays and anniversaries and when the kids come along, but each of these comes with a cross. And that's what I've noticed most: though I cherish the beautiful moments we've had, I've grown even more through the crosses.

Most of the crosses are relatively small: bills and groceries and appointments and housecleaning. But experienced in the context of marriage and family life, even those small crosses can become a heavy weight. Being late for an appointment no longer affects only me, but potentially my wife and my kids. Forgetting to get the milk used to mean I ate dry cereal, but now means midnight runs to the grocery store. And being late on a bill payment threatens not only beer money, but mortgages and insurance payments and pediatrician appointments and all the rest. Marriage forces us to see that other people rely on us, and in so doing reminds each of us just how much we rely on other people and especially on our spouses.

Sometimes that's the biggest cross. Marriage shatters the illusion that "I can do it by myself" and holds up a mirror to the rest of our lives, reminding us that no matter how hard we've worked, we didn't get to where we're at all on our own. God was with us and so were other people, often even without our knowing it. But it can be humbling to be reminded that we're not capable of everything all on our own, and it challenges our pride to have to face our very real need for other people, and especially our reliance which we can come to have on just one person—our spouse. But this is why marriage is a sacrament and why the spouses "minister" to each other. In relying on one another, we come to realize our ultimate reliance on God, and just as we grow in love and trust of our spouse, so we grow in love and trust of our God, even when it gets tough—even on the cross.

My wife and I practice Natural Family Planning. And while I could mask the difficulty in order to make it look good and more attractive, I'm not going to lie to you: NFP is *hard work*. In truth, it's probably the most difficult thing I've ever done. Certainly it's the most difficult thing that we do together as a couple. But you know what? It's also *that good*. The difficulty makes it more rewarding, and we all know that things most worth doing are often the hardest to do. So sure, it's hard sometimes having to say "No" to each other for particular reasons, but it's also really, really important. Ultimately, what we've discovered together is that every "No" we say to each other also always involves a "Yes." It can never be simply a "No, not tonight, Honey," if that "No" isn't also a "Yes" to a love which is much deeper. Sometimes that "Yes" is said aloud, but more often it's acted out in loving cuddles, in acts of kindness, or even in works of mercy.

Of course, spouses aren't the only ones who can do this. Good friends can be invaluable in helping us see where we go astray. Our parents have known us from the very beginning and can often sniff out when something is going wrong, and the older the kids get, the more they understand when we're on and when we're off. The point is that rather than be proud and refuse to take correction and advice from those who want to see us be better people, we should not only be accepting of but positively soliciting the kind of correction we need most.

Finally, the best sort of supernatural help you're going to get in this struggle to overcome yourself is going to come from the sacraments, especially Confession and Holy Communion. Pay attention to what you say every time you go to the Sacrament of Reconciliation. If you're like pretty much everyone else, you repeat yourself a lot because you tend to commit the same sins over and over and over. That's nothing to be ashamed of; in fact, it usually means that you've gotten your moral life down to where you're only struggling with one or two or three things. And if you're not going to confession enough to be able to remember what you say from one time to the next, start going more often. Father doesn't offer it daily or weekly for his own health, but for yours. How healthy do you think you'd be hitting the gym twice a year? If you really want to get over yourself, start going to confession once a month. You'll start to see the world a lot more clearly and have a lot better sense of what you really need to work on.

Beyond the particular graces that are given to spouses, kids, parents, and friends to help each other grow in holiness, there's a much more mundane and ordinary reason that the people closest to us are those best equipped to help us check our vices and practice our virtues. They live with us every day. They see us at our best and at our worst, they know what can drive us nuts and set us off, and what can stir us up and move us to action. A person can learn a lot about us simply by reading our Facebook profile or watching our online activity, but our friends and family know us in a personal, intimate, day-to-day kind of way. The trouble is, we're all running on autopilot so much of the time that our relationship with ourselves often resembles more that of the strangers who only "know" us online as opposed to our friends and family who truly know us in real life.

In order to get over ourselves, we have to start paying attention to ourselves, and if we're going to start paying attention to ourselves in the day-to-day kind of way that our friends and family already do then we have no greater tool than the Church's "Daily Examen." The *Daily Examen* is an "Examination of Conscience" or a kind of review of the day, noting the highs and lows, the mistakes and successes, and yes, the virtues and vices. Each night before you go to bed, maybe while you're getting ready for bed, maybe once in bed while you're getting ready to go to sleep, catalog your day and note what went right and what went wrong. Write it down if that's helpful or plug it into your phone or talk it over with your spouse or just note it in your head. Pay attention to trends and patterns. Notice what kinds of situations set you off and which ones make you comfortable. And pay special attention to what you do right because focusing on that is often more effective than a direct attack on particular vices. If we focus too much on what we do wrong alone, then we can wind up thinking about it more than we need to and so are often led, unintentionally, back to the same sin over and over and over again.

The other upshot to the daily examination of conscience is that it makes going to confession way easier. You don't have to try and think about the last time you went to confession, you can just kind of summarize your nightly examinations for the last three or four weeks. Then you've got both a kind of progress report on your moral life, as well as an action plan moving forward. That's why the hard work of getting over yourself is best accomplished day-by-day, right here at home, and among the people you know and love best.

QUESTIONS FOR REFLECTION

Where do I put the most time and energy in my life right now? What needs to change to make room for God?

Who are the two people in your life who would be most able to push you to grow in your faith? How might you ask them to assist you in your spiritual life?

CHAPTER SIX

ANOTHER CHRIST

The priest is not a priest for himself…he is for you.
– St. John Vianney

ONE OF THE things that surprises people most when they come to hear me speak, especially when they come to a parish mission or several presentations, is how much I talk about the priesthood. I think people are surprised to hear a layman talking in depth about the priesthood, apart from a kind of general shout-out to thank our priests for their hard work. Some people, I know, are especially surprised at how freely I talk about having been in seminary for a long time and about spending most of my early adulthood thinking I was called to a priestly vocation. I've even had people say things to me like, "Aren't you bitter that you spent all this time and have all this education, but you can't be a priest because you chose to get married?"

And the answer is, "No, not at all." Because the reason I left seminary was that the closer I got to ordination, the more I came to understand what the priesthood *really is,* and the closer I got to that reality, the more I realized that I wasn't being called to it. This decision had nothing to do with marriage, and the pope could change the discipline tomorrow, and I wouldn't be knocking on the door of any seminary. Because priesthood is its own thing, its own wonderful thing, it was only when I came to really understand the priesthood that I finally came to know what it really means to be a Christian.

Growing up, my family wasn't the best at going to Mass. That isn't to say we didn't go—we did, every single Sunday; we just weren't very good at it. Dad usually fell asleep during the homily, my mom and my sister fought and would fuss throughout, and I would spend all my time daydreaming and wondering why it was that we had to take a nap and have a fight here at church, since we seemed to do those things just fine at home. Plus, we were always late, and I do mean *always.*

Some priest had told my mother that if you could get there before the first reading that it still "counts," and she took that to heart. We were *that* family, always shuffling in at least five minutes past due, and I always prayed for a long opening song. Now that I have kids of my own, I understand why my mom was grateful for that imaginary first reading rule.

Despite consistently coming in late, however, we never, ever left early. That's because my dad has this habit that he passed on to me. After Mass, without fail, no matter where we were supposed to be or how late we were or what time the kick-off was, Dad *always* stayed to shake the priest's hand, and he made sure that I did too. As a kid, I never really understood what this obsession was all about, and as I got older, I presumed it had to do with trying to teach me to be a man and give a good, firm handshake. But when I finally thought to ask him about it, his answer floored me. "There's something about those hands, son. They're different somehow; they're *consecrated*."

And I knew immediately that what he said was true, even if it would take me years to sort out exactly what it meant. But you know what? It was only in coming to understand what he meant that I was able to know my own vocation. And to this day, my kids and I also stop to shake those *consecrated* hands.

I doubt that my dad knew it at the time, but reverencing the priest's hands is deeply rooted in our Catholic faith and practice. You've probably seen, either in movies or on TV or maybe even among recent immigrants in your own church, people bowing to *kiss* the priest's hands. This is called the *baciamano,* which is just Italian for "hand-kissing." The practice is common in cultures from Latin American to East Asia. While we might associate hand-kissing with over-the-top affection (as when a man kisses his lady's hand), or extreme submission (kissing the ring of a king or another official), the Church adopted this practice early on, but for radically different reasons.

It was common in the Roman Empire to kiss the hand of the emperor or some other civic official at the beginning or the end of a meeting. The idea was simple: good things came to you through this person, so you kissed the hands that gave you the good things. As the Church grew and developed, it recognized that the best of things come to us through the hands of our bishops and priests: the forgiveness of our sins, the healing of body and soul, and especially the Body and Blood of Christ Himself. So the practice of hand-kissing made its way into the Church and has stayed ever since. It's even official, in that in the Extraordinary Form of the Mass and in most of the Eastern Liturgies, the deacons and servers always kiss the priest's hand before handing him some sacred item or receiving it back.

Kissing the priest's hands is no longer a part of the modern liturgy, mostly because some cultures would find this gesture offensive. It's still quite common, especially with certain ethnic groups, to kiss a priest's hands upon coming or going. There's an especially beautiful tradition, which even many bishops practice, of asking a newly ordained priest for his blessing and kissing the new priest's hands immediately after his ordination. I can tell you from experience just how cool this is; you can still smell the holy oils on the man's hands—after all, they're *freshly consecrated*.

Kissing priests' hands never took off in the U.S. in the same way that it did in other countries, probably because of our suspicion of anything that seems remotely royal or hierarchical. But the intuition that there is something special about a priest's hands—the intuition that drove my dad to stick around late just to touch those hands—is really just an attempt to recognize *what a priest really is* and *why it is we need them*.

Isaac Jogues was a young Jesuit priest sent to work in the Canadian missions back in the 1630s. He and his brother Jesuits were successful in their work with the Huron people, but the nearby Iroquois were suspicious of the newly arrived "Black Robes." Eventually, they kidnapped Father Isaac, a couple of other priests, and a number of their native converts. They tortured them terribly, beating them with sticks, burning them with coals, and mutilating the priest's hands. They had noticed how the converts reverenced the hands of the priests, and so pulled out their fingernails, sawed off their thumbs, and forced the converts to gnaw off their own priest's fingers with their teeth. The pain was excruciating and the experience humiliating, but through it all Father Isaac worked hard to keep up everyone's spirits and even preached forgiveness for their captors.

Isaac was eventually ransomed and sent back to France to recuperate, where he had to receive special permission from the pope to continue to celebrate Mass with his mangled hands. Almost as soon as the permission was given, Father Isaac asked to return to the missions. At first his superiors refused his request but eventually they agreed, and he returned to America only to be shortly recaptured and ultimately martyred for the Faith.

I love the story of St. Isaac Jogues and his companions for the same reason that I love the priesthood. It's a story about real men confronting real life, pushing themselves to their limits and beyond, and showing the rest of us that we're capable of it too. St. Isaac encouraged his fellow prisoners to stay strong and faithful—not because he was a superman and they were weak—but because he knew that if he could keep it together, then his example would help them along too. He was smart and tough and creative, and he knew that he couldn't do everything he wanted to do alone. He also knew that his own judgment wasn't always the best, which is why he relied on his superiors, and even the pope, to decide when and if he were ready to return. And he did it all for Jesus because he really believed in the power of Christ at work in the Church and especially in the sacraments. And by living out what he believed in, Father Isaac showed us why he loved the priesthood so much, and why we should love it too.

The natives who murdered Fr. Isaac and his companions were confused about what was happening. They saw the reverence the Christian converts paid to the priest's hands and thought it was some kind of strange magic. They thought that if you could get rid of the fingers, you would get rid of the magic. But the problem is that the power wasn't in the hands; it was in the man, and yet it wasn't the man's own power, it was God's. So when they cut off the priest's hands, they only made him *more powerful,* and when they finally put him to death, they gave both Fr. Isaac and the Church *life*—a new kind of life they couldn't possibly imagine. And Father Isaac's legacy proved this. Within a year the French had captured Isaac's killer and condemned him to death, but while still a captive and awaiting execution, the man asked to be baptized. He chose to be renamed Isaac Jogues, in honor of the martyr he had made.

St. Isaac was, to the natives whom he served, an *alter Christus*, another Christ. This is the fundamental role of the priest, to serve as a sign of Christ's presence in the Christian community—the Church—and to act on Christ's behalf in sanctifying, teaching, and governing His people. St. Isaac took this to its logical conclusion and wound up dying for the Faith he had come to preach, just as Jesus did. But every priest in the world, from the pope on down to the assistant in your own parish has this same mission: to *be Christ* for those the Church sends him to serve.

Of course, this would be impossible all on one's own. That's why the Church *ordains* her ministers: bishops, priests, and deacons, all for different service within the community. Each is empowered to fulfill his own particular function. When a man is ordained a priest, the bishop prays:

> Together with us,
> May they be faithful stewards of your mysteries,
> So that your people may be renewed in the waters of rebirth
> And nourished from your altar;
> So that sinners may be reconciled

And the sick raised up.
May they be joined with us, Lord,
In imploring your mercy
For the people entrusted to their care
And for all the world (*Roman Pontifical,* 131).

The priest is the primary minister of the Church for most of us. The parish priest baptizes and preaches, marries and buries, hears our confessions and celebrates the Eucharist for us. As the above prayer says, he both stands as Christ for us and stands before Christ on our behalf. This is the dynamic at the heart of the priesthood: to go from the people to God with their prayers, concerns, and struggles, and to return to the people from God with His grace-filled gifts.

The Church has a special name for the role which the priest has in administering the sacraments. He is said to act *in persona Christi,* or, *in the person of Christ.* This is because:

It is the same priest, Christ Jesus, whose sacred person his minister truly represents. Now the minister, by reason of the sacerdotal [priestly] consecration which he has received, is truly made like to the high priest and possesses the authority to act in the power and place of the person of Christ himself. (*CCC,* 1548).

The priest acts *in the person of Christ* because he has been ordained to do so. His ordination confers a very real power, a power I can't claim to possess and which nobody in his right mind would ever dare to claim. It can only be given, as in Holy Orders; but even there it isn't for the priest's own benefit, but for the sake of those he is sent to serve. So the priest is able to say, "This is my body," and be sure that God has made it so, not because the priest is especially smart or holy, but because God has empowered him to do so—*for us*. And in so doing, the priest reveals not only what's special about his life and work, but what God has in store for us too.

You see, the priest not only acts *in persona Christi*, but *in persona Christi* **capitis**; *in the person of Christ* **the head**. The head of what? Well of His body, the Church. St. Paul sings about this in the Letter to the Colossians:

> *He* [Christ] *is the image of the invisible God,*
> *the firstborn of all creation.*
> *For in him were created all things in heaven and on earth,*
> *the visible and the invisible,*
> *whether thrones or dominions or principalities or powers;*
> *all things were created through him and for him.*
>
> *He is before all things,*
> *and in him all things hold together.*
> *He is the head of the body, the church.*
> *He is the beginning, the firstborn from the dead,*
> *that in all things he himself might be preeminent.*
>
> *For in him all the fullness was pleased to dwell,*
> *and through him to reconcile all things for him,*

making peace by the blood of his cross
[through him], *whether those on earth or those in heaven.*
(Col. 1:15-20)

The priest serves *in the person of Christ the Head* in order to remind us of who we are because of our baptism: *in persona Christi corporis; in the person of Christ* **the Body**. The Church *really* is the Body of Christ, but a body without a head is no body at all. It's without direction, can't sustain itself, and ultimately won't be able to accomplish its mission. Priests have a special purpose and are empowered to do amazing, even impossible things, but that power comes with great responsibility. *We* are that great responsibility, which means that we must have something pretty powerful going on too.

I went to seminary and pursued, for a long time, what I thought was a vocation to the priesthood because I recognized in the priests I knew something good, something holy, and something immensely powerful. While I was at seminary I lived with, learned from, and grew under the direction of some of the finest priests in the world. Each day my admiration for them as individual men and for the priesthood they shared grew and grew. At the same time, I came to know them in a much more human way than most people ever do. I saw them in their cassocks and in their pajamas, standing at the altar and running on the basketball court, studying theology in the classroom and arguing over a favorite show in the TV room. And I saw them struggle after the death of a parent, through a difficult assignment, in their relationships with each other, and with their own tendency to sin. But in the midst of all of this humanity, and oftentimes because of it, I saw grace shine through even in the midst of frailty. I saw God work in them and through them for their own sake, and for the sake of those they served.

The Fathers of Vatican II realized the same thing. That's why they wrote:

> They [the bishops and priests] also know that they were not ordained by Christ to take upon themselves alone the entire salvific mission of the Church toward the world. On the contrary they understand that it is their noble duty to shepherd the faithful and to recognize their ministries and charisms, so that all according to their proper roles may cooperate in this common undertaking with one mind (*Lumen Gentium*, 30).

This "common undertaking" is the mission from God on which we've all been sent. Don't think you've been given a mission from God? Thought that only belonged to priests and other "holy folk"? Think again. When you were baptized, literally just after they wiped the water off your head, the priest anointed you with oil—the same oil a priest is ordained with—and said this:

God the Father of our Lord Jesus Christ has freed you from sin and given you a new birth by water and the Holy Spirit. He now anoints with the chrism of salvation. As Christ was anointed Priest, Prophet, and King, so may you live always as a member of His body, sharing everlasting life. Amen *(Rite of Baptism)*.

From the moment of your baptism, you were given a mission, or better, a share in the mission of the Church. And that mission is nothing less than the salvation of the whole world.

The lay apostolate, however, is a participation in the salvific mission of the Church itself. Through their baptism and confirmation all are commissioned to that apostolate by the Lord Himself. Moreover, by the sacraments, especially holy Eucharist, that charity toward God and man which is the soul of the apostolate is communicated and nourished. Now the laity are called in a special way to make the Church present and operative in those places and circumstances where only through them can it become the salt of the earth. Thus every lay person, in virtue of the very gifts bestowed upon him, is at the same time a witness and a living instrument of the mission of the Church itself "according to the measure of Christ's bestowal" (*Lumen Gentium*, 33).

By our baptism and confirmation, and by every Mass we ever attend, we are sent on mission for Christ. In fact, the very word "Mass" means "The Sending." At the end of Mass, when the priest or deacon acclaims, "Go forth, the Mass is ended," what he's really saying is, "Get out there and get to work. We've given you what you need to get it done, now let's roll up our sleeves and get to it." The mission of the ordained is to sanctify the Church; the mission of the laity is to sanctify the world.

Part of the attraction of priesthood for me, and for a lot of guys, is the "otherness" of it all. They wear special clothes, not just on duty but off. They don't marry or have families of their own, which singles (pun intended) them out as particularly dedicated to their work. They receive a lot of respect, even if people aren't kissing their hands, and they do extraordinary work. They're special, not in the superficial way that people told us when we were kids, but in a very real, tangible, even public sense. There's something different, something other, something holy about the priesthood—even if each individual priest struggles with holiness just as much as you and I do.

What I did not realize and what I think most of us don't realize is that simply being baptized—living an ordinary Catholic life—is just as special. And again, I don't mean this "special" in the cheap, participation certificate sort of way. The priests of the Church live "other" sorts of lives *in order to remind us* of the "otherness" to which we're all called. We could have a totally functional sort of ministry in the Church–bishops, priests, and deacons who simply perform particular functions and administer the proper sacraments, but instead the Church forms, shapes, and directs the lives of her ministers around their life in the Church.

But it is not *only* the priests who are to model their lives on the mystery of the cross; that calling belongs to all of us. The priests are simply called upon to do it in a more radical, public sort of way, as a sign and an inspiration to the rest of us to do what they're trying to do—get over themselves and live for Christ. This is what St. Isaac Jogues was doing with the natives in Canada and what your parish priest is doing just around the corner.

In that hymn I quoted earlier from Colossians, Jesus is called the *eikon*, the *image* of the invisible God. As the Church developed her own tradition of artwork, the icon came to have pride of place. You've seen them before, and though they're common in Eastern Christian churches, most regular Catholic Churches have them as well. They're flat, two-dimensional, highly stylized kind of paintings. They are astounding in their beauty and have their own complex symbolism. But the idea of the *icon* is this: we are not so much seeing the icon and thinking about who or what the image represents (Jesus, Mary, one of the saints, or an image from the Bible), but rather *looking through* the icon to the reality which it calls to mind.

Our ordained ministers are *living icons*. They each have their own special symbolism, made up of the particular way that the grace of Holy Orders works itself out in the life of the individual, but they all lead us to see *through* them and catch a glimpse of Christ. Deacons, in a particular way, stand for Christ as a servant. That's why they always stand to the right of the priest or bishop, ready to assist them with whatever they're doing. Both priests and bishops stand for *Christ the head*, exercising leadership and direction over the Body of Christ, the Church. Priests, in a particular way, and especially parish priests, remind me of *Christ the Victim*. As they bow before the host and say, "This is my body," they're doing so in the name of Christ. But just as each of us is called to offer our lives with the offering on the altar, so is the individual priest, and if he does it well, if he means it and tries to integrate it into his life, *then he offers his life too*. That is, after all, the whole point of priestly ordination—to lay down one's life for the sake of Christ and His Church.

For me, one of the greatest signs of this happens at a man's ordination, just before the moment of ordination itself. The bishop, in order to prepare himself and the man to be ordained, invites everyone present to kneel and face the altar. The man to be ordained lies prostrate on the ground—flat on his face—while the whole assembly chants the great Litany of the Saints. In those final moments before being given the power to do the impossible so that he might give everything he has in service to Christ, the man *literally lays down his life*. It's the most vulnerable posture imaginable; people could literally walk all over him if they wanted to, but instead the man is held up by the prayers of those present, both living and dead. As the Church invokes the intercession of the saints—

those who have succeeded in laying down their lives—this both strengthens the man's resolve, and provides him with models to imitate in his new way of life.

Priestly ordinations are remarkable events. They're full of rich ceremony and symbolism, and they can be kind of overwhelming. But what's craziest about all of this is that the guy being ordained is literally your brother or son or friend. We all know that "priests are people too," but it becomes strikingly real when the guy lying on the floor, having the saints invoked over him played racquetball with you yesterday or took your sister to the senior prom or used to fight with you over toys or TV time. God chooses ordinary men, really, truly, ordinary men, for positively *extraordinary* work.

One of my favorite examples of an ordinary man who wound up called to an extraordinary mission is Miguel Pro. Miguel was an ordinary kid from an ordinary family in Mexico. He was apparently somewhat mischievous and loved to play practical jokes on his brothers and sisters. He was popular with the girls and always assumed he'd work in his father's business, but when his older sister unexpectedly entered the convent, he started discerning a religious vocation himself.

He entered the Jesuits and was sent to study in Spain, but while he was in Spain, Mexico enacted some of the harshest anti-Catholic political campaigns since the Reformation. Priests and religious couldn't present themselves in public (wear collars or habits); they were forbidden to vote or sit on juries; the Church's property and resources were all seized by the government, and the local authorities could determine the number of priests allowed to be in a given area at any one time. Now Miguel had a problem. He had a stomach problem and needed to relocate back to Mexico, but while in Spain he'd been ordained a priest, and the Mexican government wouldn't allow him back into the country, even though he was a Mexican citizen.

So he had to sneak back into the country where he carried out a secret ministry to Catholics who no longer had access to their priests. This secrecy went on for nearly three years, but eventually he was discovered. Rather than deporting him, the Mexican government chose to make an example out of him and trumped-up charges that he was plotting to assassinate the president. He was executed without trial and went to his death yelling, *"Viva Cristo Rey!"* or "Long live Christ the King!"

These final words became the rallying cry of the Cristero Revolutionaries who worked to restore freedom to the Church in Mexico, and while their campaign was successful, the Church's freedoms weren't fully restored in Mexico until the 1990s. It's easy to imagine that Miguel, now *Blessed Miguel Pro, SJ,* was responsible for at least some of that success from heaven.

The real power of Bl. Miguel's story for me, however, isn't that yet another brave priest died for the Faith under an oppressive government. What I love about Miguel is that, in most ways, he was pretty unremarkable. He was reasonably bright, but not super-smart. He liked soccer, but wasn't very good at it, and he loved his pranks and jokes, which sometimes were funny and sometimes were just plain annoying. He was, basically, your kid brother or your goofy uncle or the guy who lives next door. And yet he did remarkable things every day of his life and ultimately died a remarkable death—a death that reminds us—*all of us* that *our lives are ultimately not about us.*

Miguel Pro exemplifies exactly what a priest should be. He's a reminder—a powerful reminder—of the extraordinary breaking through into the ordinary. He shows us in his life and in his death how the rough hands of a plumber or a carpenter can call down God's Spirit from heaven, how the whispered words of an English teacher or a football coach can accomplish the work of Christ's forgiveness, how the wrinkled hands and raspy voice of a man who could be your grandfather can give comfort, rest, and peace to the sick and the dying. Miguel reminds us of all that's good and right and wonderful about the priesthood; that through it, through our own brothers who are willing to get over themselves, sacrificing their lives, God chooses to save us, and in so doing, enables us to help save the world.

QUESTIONS FOR REFLECTION

In what ways have the priests in my life been an icon of Christ for me?

How does my regular celebration of the Eucharist call me to be an icon of Christ for others?

CHAPTER SEVEN

The (Second) Greatest Gift to Conquer the World's Greatest Sin

God forgives a repentant sinner his sins faster than a mother can pull her child out of the fire.

– St. John Vianney

I T's BEEN SAID that if Christ hadn't given Confession to the Church that doctors or psychologists or even judges would have had to invent it themselves. We are *confessing beings*; we don't like keeping secrets, especially about ourselves, and secret shame messes us up in a way that ordinary guilt does not. Jesus works *with our nature* in the Sacrament of Reconciliation—not against it.

Confession is good for the soul; it allows us to clear our consciences and bare our souls, and it forces us to act humble even if we're not really feeling it much in the moment. Why? Because it allows another person, a third party, to hold up a mirror so that we can see what we really look like *from the inside out*. Simply put, if you really want to conquer your pride and get over yourself, then you won't find a better weapon than Confession.

It's funny, the thing that people worry about most when it comes to Confession—whether Catholic or Protestant—is having to confess their sins to another person. *Why do I have to confess my sins to a priest? Why can't I just go directly to God?* Well, the sacrament itself presumes that you have gone directly to God, and God has moved you so much that you recognize the need to go to the sacrament. It's funny because, like little kids complaining about their vegetables, the complaints about Confession are, of course, about the part that makes it good for us.

Historically speaking, we might just flip the question around. *How come I **get** to confess my sins **only** to the priest?* The reason that I say that is because in the early Church Confession was done in public. Now by "public" I do not mean in the way that it is "public" now—how you can see who else is going to Confession by the line outside the door or in the "Confession Marathons" that some places host when there are several priests hearing Confessions all at the same time. No, in the early Church, you made your Confession in front of everybody—to the priest or more likely to the bishop and to the whole congregation gathered there with him. And instead of being given absolution and then sent off to "do your penance" or make restitution, the penance was given and had to be completed *before* you could be absolved—because *doing the penance* was—and still is—part of the process of forgiveness. Working the steps helped to bring you back into right relationship with God and with your neighbor, so that when the time came for you to receive the absolution you would be ready for it.

Now part of the reason for public Confession in the early Church was that the sins being confessed were more serious and generally more public sins. If you, say, slept with someone's wife, then that act has public consequences, whether or not you were caught. Why? Because you and she have done damage to her marriage and to yours (if you're married too), and so both of your spouses and your kids and your other relationships are affected—whether or not you realize it. So you would confess publicly and do your penance, and the penance would be tough (no two *Our Fathers*, three *Hail Marys*, and a *Glory Be* for this one), but then once it was done, it was done. You were then *publicly reconciled* just as you had *publicly confessed*.

Now the idea of confessing your secret sins publicly to a group of strangers or at least to a group of almost-strangers, and then entrusting your moral growth to another person and the support of a tight-knit community probably sounds terrifying and seems kind of crazy to most of us today. That is, unless of course, we attend AA, NA, GA, SA, SLA, OA, or any of the other "Anonymous" groups which meet at churches and schools and community centers all around the world every night of the year. Alcoholics Anonymous and the various groups that have spun off from it have helped literally millions of people overcome addiction, and they are based on the same kind of model as Confession in the Catholic Church. Even for those of us who don't necessarily struggle with addictions, but struggle through the moral life in ordinary sorts of ways, third-party accountability can be one of the best ways not just to get over the sin but to get over the pride that's tied to hiding it.

That's no accident; the Church has sponsors too. That's why we have godparents who "stand up" for us and with our parents at our baptism—if we're baptized as infants; it's also why the people who vouch for us at Confirmation are actually called *sponsors*. In many cultures, the witnesses at a person's wedding—what we might think of as the best man and maid/matron of honor—are the godparents of the couple getting married. And, of course, when we come to Confession, the sponsor is our confessor. This is also why, as best as we're able, we should try and go to the same priest regularly. Over time he'll get to know our regular sins and our basic patterns, the things that can set us off and hold us back as well as those things that can help us internally reset and get back on track. He can help us keep track of our growth, so that it doesn't always seem as if we're just making the same mistakes over and over again. Nothing works more against our own growth in the spiritual life than a constant sense that we aren't and can't move forward.

When I was a kid, I loved my Transformers. If you weren't into them then or if your kids never were, then you might know them from the movies that came out over the last few years. Essentially, they were toys that were shaped initially like cars. But with a few cleverly hidden hinges and springs, these cars could be *transformed* into impressive-looking robots. Some of them could even transform into yet another thing: a boat, a planet, a rocket. What I loved about them, though, was that when looking at this little car, you'd never imagine there was a person inside. Or, the other way around, you'd never know looking at this person-shaped robot that it had the potential to become a car.

Each of us is a little like a transformer. We all have untapped potential, and not only in the sense that we're all capable of more than we give ourselves credit for, though that's usually true. No, we all have the potential; yes, really, *we all have the potential **to become saints**.* That chubby dad with the unshaven beard and the crying kid at the grocery store has the potential to stand next to the martyr in the stained-glass window. Your boss at work who can be so short and angry and is struggling to raise three kids on her own has the potential to look out at you from an icon like one of the saints of old. The people who live with you: your spouse who spends too much money, your kid who can't get off his phone, your sister who never listens, and your dad who is unintentionally offensive all have a real shot at sainthood.

The problem is that there's a huge gap between most of us ordinary dads and the saints we're meant to be. The crabby lady at work or the angst-filled teen or the grumpy old man all still have a lot of growing up to do; and that growing up is mostly a matter of getting over ourselves. The thing about the Transformers was that though the hinges and springs were always there, you had to play with them a while before they slid easily into place. And at first one form tended to come more easily than the other; either the robot would stand lopsided or the car wouldn't quite run straight.

The same is true for us: our hinges need oiled and our springs sprung. We have to practice virtues before we can acquire them; we have to pray like saints before we're even close to being saints ourselves. And most of all, we have to be open to the possibility that God sees something in us that we can't yet see ourselves. The action of God working out that possibility in us is what we call *grace*.

And that's why the Sacrament of Reconciliation is more than an AA meeting or a therapy session or spiritual direction. It's got graces available that we just can't get anywhere else, and those graces have the ability to transform not only our interaction with the priest in the confessional, but our weekly AA meetings or our sessions with our therapist or spiritual direction or sharing a problem with a friend or struggling through a relationship with a spouse. The graces of the sacrament forgive us our sins absolutely, but they do more than that. If we're open to it, they can *transform* our whole lives: eating and sleeping and working and praying and playing and all the rest into occasions to grow in holiness, moments to meet God.

If you want to lose weight in a hurry, you can just stop eating. But it won't get you very far, and before long you'll have gained it all back. If you want to lose weight more permanently, you've got to change your lifestyle. You've got to eat, but eat better than you did before, and you've got to exercise in order to burn up the calories that you're taking in. Diet alone won't do it and neither will exercise; the one will mess up your metabolism, and the other, while it might trim your waistline, will actually make you heavier as you build up more muscle. If you want to make lasting changes, you've got to change what goes in and what *comes out.*

Our spiritual lives are no different. Lasting change demands altering our lifestyle; we have to adjust both exercise and diet. This chapter has been addressing a kind of spiritual regimen; a confessor is really like a personal trainer in the spiritual life. But on its own, spiritual squats and lunges will only make you capable of doing more with what you've already got. To see things really change, you've got to eat differently—both *what* you eat and *how* you eat it.

The bottom line is that frequent confession is not enough. Yes, you read that right: *frequent confession.* The Church demands Confession at least once a year, but doing the bare minimum is never going to get you to greatness. Even twice a year during Advent and Lent is hardly enough. If you were really struggling with something emotionally, then you'd go to your therapist to work it out at least once a month, probably every week or two. Confession is just the same: aim for once a month, and then, as you start to grow, figure out what pattern works best for you.

As I said, frequent Confession is like a prerequisite to this kind of growth, but it's not enough on its own. That's why I titled this chapter "The Second Greatest Weapon" because there's a bigger gun yet. Together they are unstoppable in the struggle to get over yourself. That "World's Greatest Weapon," that "Magic Bullet," that "Secret You've Always Been Looking For" was right under your nose all along; it's called "Holy Communion."

Regular Confession needs to always be accompanied by frequent Communion. *This* is the Greatest Gift, the Best Defense, the one and only Ace in the Hole to get over yourself and on to the life God wants you to live. A "Good Communion," one that we've thought about ahead of time, prepared for as best as we can, and that we receive as humbly and honestly as we can, will do more than a thousand therapy sessions or spiritual directions or anything else. We sometimes treat the Holy Eucharist like it's some kind of divine vitamin pill, but this is something much, much more. Holy Communion realigns our passions, resets our hopes and our dreams, makes up for and heals what is broken in us and builds on what is already good. Too often we see Confession and Communion only in terms of preparation and consumption—like going on a diet-cleanse before beginning a new exercise routine. It's much more like getting on the diet-and-exercise regimen we'd always meant to but simply had never gotten to before.

It's certainly true that you need to prepare for Holy Communion, and that probably most of us don't do as good a job of this as we could. If you're so sick to your stomach that you can't hold anything down, then you're not ready to take your medicine yet. But you don't have to be 100 percent better to start taking your pills either—otherwise there would be no point in taking the medicine at all.

I have a priest friend who's also a science nerd who says that "Confession and Communion are spiritually symbiotic; they depend upon one another for each other to work well." They riff off each other, strengthen and support one another, and like diet and exercise, *both are essential* to living a healthy, holy life—to becoming the men and women God has always longed for us to be—fully *transformed* in Christ.

QUESTIONS FOR REFLECTION

How often do I go to Confession? How could I go more often or get more out of it?

How do I prepare to receive Holy Communion? How could I better utilize the sacramental gifts that God has given me?

CHAPTER EIGHT

HOW TO ACT

Love God, serve God; everything is in that.

– St. Clare of Assisi

A MAN ONCE approached Mother Teresa and said, "I don't understand why you think you can do this kind of work better than government social workers." In response she invited him to come and spend a day with her. He stayed a week. At the end of it all, he told her, "Now I understand. Our social workers, even many of the Christians, do their work for *something*. You and your sisters do your work for Some*one*."

On the face of it, Christian service can look pretty similar to the Boy Scouts or Habitat for Humanity or even the Shriners. We raise money for worthy causes, do nice things for people, and pay special attention to the less fortunate and those who can't help themselves. But authentic Christian service is something different, something unique, and it's rooted in our personal relationship with Jesus. And as we know from St. John, our relationship with Jesus didn't start with us but with Him. *"We love because he first loved us"* (1 John 4:19)—loved us into being, loved us even after our sinful fall, and loves us still—even in the daily struggle which we wage to get over and stay over ourselves. How could we not return that love with love in worship and service?

Other religions certainly make moral demands on their people, and God had already revealed some of what was to become so clear in Jesus to the people of Israel before He ever showed up. But while the Buddha recommends acts of loving kindness in order to detach further from our desires, we Christians grow in desire—the desire to love more and serve better than we ever have before. And though the gods of Greece and Rome occasionally gave shout-outs to widows and orphans and immigrants, they also commanded the deaths of deformed babies and established slavery as an institution of divine right. At the story's end, even Odin, the All-Father of the Norse Pantheon, who was sacrificed on a tree and pierced with a spear like Jesus, was a liar and a trickster and a bloodthirsty tyrant. When these gods commanded service, it was always *for them—for their own sake*—to add to their prominence or to appease their wants. But the service which the God and Father of Jesus demands, the service which Jesus showed us perfectly how to offer, isn't because He needs it, but because He knows it's best for us.

Jesus flipped the script: though sinless, He insisted on being baptized; He appointed leaders from among working class laborers and hung out with prostitutes and criminals; He offered Himself in service to them and allows them to offer service in return; and in the most stunning example of service ever offered, He took on the role of the least of slaves and washes His disciples' feet. *"You call me 'teacher' and 'master,' and rightly so, for indeed I am. If I, therefore, the master and teacher, have washed your feet, you ought to wash one another's feet"* (John 13:13, 14). And then He backs this symbolic action with the most practical thing anyone has ever done. He offers *Himself* as a sacrifice *for us.* That's the model for all other Christian service—to offer ourselves on behalf of other people.

We already know the story, so sometimes this doesn't quite have the dramatic effect which was originally intended. But it's easy to see, given how different Jesus was from everyone around Him and how much He challenged people's ideas and even their unspoken prejudices, why it took His disciples so long to figure out what was going on. We give poor Peter a hard time in the gospel for getting it wrong so often, but believe me, I wouldn't want to have to stand in his place. I'm still getting it wrong today, and I not only know the end of the story (which Peter didn't), but have had two thousand years of good examples to follow on top of it. And here's the good news: so have you.

Service is at the heart of the gospel and at the heart of what it means to be a Catholic, but you MUST hear what I'm saying. The kind of service I'm talking about isn't simply social work or volunteering for good causes, though those are all good and might even reflect the deeper life of service which we're aiming at. But Christian service is about more than politeness and social awareness; it's not simply holding open doors for people and waving people through traffic, giving money to flood victims and keeping up with the news.

The kind of service Jesus calls us to is not that simple, and it's certainly not nearly so easy.

St. Paul captures the dynamic of Christian service when he writes, *"Indeed, only with difficulty does one die for a just person, though perhaps for a good person one might even find courage to die. But God proves his love for us in that while we were still sinners Christ died for us"* (Rom. 5:7-8). The astounding thing isn't that Christ died for His friends—lots of people do that—but that He died for the very people who were putting Him to death.

An ancient tradition tells us that the centurion in charge of the soldiers who were crucifying Jesus was nearly blind. When he ordered the spear to be thrust through Christ's side and the blood and water came pouring out, some touched his eyes and he was healed. *"Father, forgive them, they know not what they do,"* wasn't just poetry for Jesus; He was literally saving those who put Him to death.

So we are called not simply to tolerate our enemies, not just to ignore them or try not to think about them or avoid getting into fights with them. No, we're called to LOVE them and to show that love in acts of service. But what is love? St. Thomas Aquinas says that to love another person is to desire their true good and work toward it. So Jesus is calling us to both WANT and WORK for their good on a continual basis. In fact, He's already given us the criteria by which we are to be judged. *"The measure with which you measure will be measured out to you,"* and in another place, *"Whatever you did for these least of mine, you did to me."*

The people who are least in your life are most likely not the untouchables of Calcutta or the starving orphans of Ethiopia. No, the least people in your life are the members of your own family you simply can't stand, the brother who bankrupted your parents with rehab but never got sober, the aunt who drove your cousin out of the house, or the grandfather who just never seems satisfied with anything. They're the co-worker you loathe because his politics are opposite yours, the opinionated neighbor you complain about to your spouse, or the cashier you always avoid at the grocery store because her breath stinks. *These* are the least among you; *these* are Jesus—for you. I often wonder, and sometimes fear, if at the final judgment Jesus will appear as the person I struggled with most in life.

Sometimes I think we imagine that Mother Teresa *enjoyed* cleaning up after the sick and the poor, or that St. Damien *liked* the puss-ridden sores and rotting limbs of the lepers on Molokai. The truth is that they *loved* the people they tended to, but they didn't love the poverty, and they certainly didn't love the disease. Those things were hard for them—just as they'd be hard for you or for me, but they were able to do it because, over time, they'd *gotten over themselves enough* to see past the sickness and serve in love. They'd grown mature enough spiritually to give themselves over—in even the most difficult of circumstances, *because they loved so much.*

This love moved both of them out of very comfortable lives

into some of the most uncomfortable circumstances imaginable. Before she founded the Missionaries of Charity, Mother Teresa taught at an elite girls' school in Darjeeling. And before he asked to be sent to the lepers in the South Pacific, Fr. Damien lived comfortably in Belgium. But they chose to put themselves out and go the extra mile. Mother Teresa risked everything to found a new kind of religious order which now, decades after her death, is still among the fastest-growing in the world. Fr. Damien moved to Molokai and never left, willingly accepting a lifetime of quarantine exile, and ultimately succumbing to the very disease he'd come to try to help people recover from. But both were able to do this because their dedication was not to a cause or an ideal. They weren't devoted to "eradicating poverty" as a principle or "making leprosy a thing of the past" as a slogan. They were devoted to a person, Jesus Christ, and in light of that devotion gave themselves in loving service to other people because love moves us out of ourselves and helps us to *go out of our way* for the sake of the other.

That's what's so compelling about the lives of the saints. It's not that they simply waited around for people to need things and then supplied them as they came. Even the hermits of the desert extended themselves for other people. Christians *put themselves out there* for love, and the love which moves them to do so can move mountains, change lives, and ultimately bring the dead back to life. And even though this love is authentically humble, not puffed up or interested in itself, it is potent and virile. It's the kind of love that makes saints and that pushes people out of their comfort zones and into the deep waters of life, of heartbreak, of danger and adventure, of hopes and of dreams and ultimately, of God.

Of course, you don't have to be a priest or religious to give yourself in loving service like that, and you don't have to move to a foreign country to put yourself out there for the gospel. There are plenty of opportunities to serve right where you are: in your very own neighborhood, parish, city, or town. Poor people are everywhere who need a helping hand and probably even more people who are poor in spirit in need of a friend, a true friend, to bring them to God. That's the real key to the beatitude, *"Blessed are the poor."* They're not blessed because poverty is good, but because God loves them, and in loving them, we grow to love God the more. This is especially true, not only for those who can't afford to pay their bills, but for those who have trouble getting out of bed in the morning, those crippled by sadness and loneliness and pain, those held back by longheld hurts and ancient griefs and grudges. These are the people—and we all know them—most in need of the care of the Church and most in need of our loving service.

I've been to a lot of churches—probably you've been to some too—where the pews are half-empty, and everyone wonders why. They blame the preaching, which usually could be better or the music which often isn't great or the parking lot which could be bigger or the building which could be fixed up a bit. I once even heard a person say that the reason the church was empty was because the kneelers were too uncomfortable, as though if everything else was running perfectly, the kneelers would be enough to keep people away!

These are all good things to think about, but these aren't the reasons people really leave church—even if they're the excuses people often give. No, the reason that your church is nearly empty is staring you right in the face; just look in the mirror, squint if you have to—it's you and me. That might sound harsh, and I don't mean it personally, but I'm also not the first person to propose that reason.

G. K. Chesterton, one of the greatest Catholics of the twentieth century, wrote a book in 1910 called *What's Wrong with the World*. He spends about two hundred pages listing off all of the horrible things happening around the world and then comes to this startling conclusion: "It's me, I'm what's wrong with the world." Now if you know anything about Chesterton, it's not that he had problems with self-esteem. It's just that he realized what most of us don't or at least what we most often forget; I contribute to the evil that's in the world, and so it's my obligation to work hard for what is good.

We talk today about offsetting our carbon footprint; well, Chesterton understood that we have to offset our "sinful footprint" by cultivating virtue and living lives of service. Why? Not because God's an accountant with a heavenly bank statement keeping track of our deposits and withdrawals. Rather, growing in virtue and living lives of service habituates us, disposes us, *trains us* to desire the good and work toward it, *to get over ourselves and get on with the business of loving God and our neighbor as best as we possibly can.*

Think for a moment about how many elderly people live in your parish who would love to come to Mass on Sunday, but they have no one to drive them. You've got four extra seats in your car that are going unused. What do you think would happen if you asked Father for a list of those who need a ride? And if just five other people did the same thing? Right! That would be four pews filled on Sunday that right now are sitting empty. Or what about your cousin who doesn't come to Mass anymore? It's because he's living with his girlfriend, right? WRONG. He is living with his girlfriend, and he suspects that's not probably the best situation for him, but he's embarrassed to come back to Church because he feels like people will judge him. What would happen if you invited him? Or what about your priest who is shuffling between two parishes and doesn't get time to eat on Sunday. That last Mass is his third or even fourth of the weekend, and he's always obviously tired and low on energy. What would happen if you offered to bring food for him between Masses so that he could recharge and then have more energy for his later Mass?

Of course, each of these means putting yourself out (which really is the entire point of this book) in demanding acts of loving service. Each of these means pushing our boundaries and trying something—something uncomfortable—and we don't have any guarantee regarding the consequences. Maybe the old people in your car will be crabby and complain about your driving. Maybe your cousin will tell you he has no use for religion, and he thinks you're silly for still going to church. Maybe your priest will be such a fussy eater that after the first week, it's clear this isn't going to work. But one thing's for sure: if you don't try, your church will still be empty, and you'll still be part of the problem rather than the solution.

I know how hard this all sounds, believe me, and I don't pretend to be perfect on this score—not by a long shot. I know that this can sound preachy and judgmental, and I get why some of my suggestions might seem impossible given your particular circumstances. But I do know two things. First, it wasn't until I really took a chance and started putting myself out there in this way that things started to really come alive in my own spiritual life. And second, if we're going to be a Church after the heart of Jesus, if we're going to be a Church of Love, then we must act, and we must act soon.

QUESTIONS FOR REFLECTION

What is one act of service I can commit to each week for one year?

What steps could you take this month to strengthen the life of your parish?

CHAPTER NINE

FUNNY THING

Leave sadness to those in the world. We who work for God should be lighthearted.

— St. Leonard of Port Maurice

I KNOW A priest who is a renowned exorcist—one of the most sought after in the world—and we were talking one day about evil and how it works in our lives. I asked, "Given all of the resources which the Church gives us, what's our best defense against the Devil?"

His answer startled me. I was expecting him to say something pious like "the rosary" or "Eucharistic Adoration" or something like that. Instead he smiled and said simply, "Humor. Satan hates to be mocked."

It makes sense when you think about it. The bad angels fell because of pride, and nothing cuts the prideful down to size—whether human beings or angels—like being reminded of just who and what you really are. The Devil is a liar and a fake; he mimics God, but the best he can manage are pale imitations. And so he hates it when we know the truth and toss it back in his face; he has no ultimate power over us, we have been baptized, washed in the blood of the Lamb, sealed with the Gift of the Spirit, marked for the day of eternity. Demons are real and are nothing to be fooled with, but the victory is already ours; demons are like troops who haven't gotten word that the war is over, and they've already lost—or better yet, they've gotten the memo, know the score, and keep on fighting anyway—for spite, for pride, and for hate.

Humor and humility are not two words we often pair together, but they are rooted in the same reality, which makes them effective antidotes against both pride and hate. The origin of both words is the same, the Latin *umor* meaning "earth," or perhaps better, "dirt." *Humor* and *humility* both serve to ground us; they remind us of who we are and where we've come from and where it is we're going, which helps us to see things as they actually are. It's easy to get lost in the falsehoods in our heads: who we think we should be, where we should be from, what other people expect from us, and how we'd rather the world really be; but these are all Satan's traps—they're tricks designed to make us think that we aren't enough just as we are, and that no one, not even God, could love us with all our faults. The lies we tell ourselves are truly *diabolical*, they divide us against ourselves and make it easier for the enemy to conquer.

So from the very beginning, the saints of the Church have held humor to be both one of God's greatest gifts and one of our greatest resources. Plenty of comics are running around today and whole TV networks are dedicated to comedy, but they don't give humor even half the credit that we Christians do. For most people, jokes are an escape, silliness is just a salve for the inevitable pains of life and living, but for the Christian they are much, much more. For the Christian to laugh is something divine, and humor provides us with a lens to see the world as it really is—with all the gunk, and all the grace rolled up together in one.

"Angels can fly," G. K. Chesterton wrote, "because they take themselves lightly. It is easy to be heavy; hard to be light. Satan fell by force of gravity." The Christian life is all about learning how to fly.

Chesterton, who was one of the best defenders of the Faith in the twentieth century, wrote a lot about humor, which was good because he was a pretty funny guy in his own right. But he noted the humor present in the lives of the saints and had the ability to see humor where other people might be more inclined to see something else. In his famous biography of St. Francis of Assisi he wrote, "The sense of humor *salts* all his escapades." The play on words was deliberate; Jesus called His disciples to be salt and light, and St. Francis used that imagery to form his band of merry friars. But he did so precisely with *humor*, with earthiness, and with an eye set firmly on humility and the lifelong task of getting over himself.

For example, many are familiar with the scene of Francis at the bishop's house. Francis' father is angry because his son has been giving away too much stuff, and he wants the bishop to get involved and stop Francis before he bankrupts the family. Francis famously strips himself naked right there in front of everybody, places the clothes at his father's feet and declares that he no longer has an earthly father—only a Heavenly One. The bishop then took off his own cope and covered Francis with it. Now when this scene is usually shown or recounted, Francis is supposed to be showcasing his humility—the original humble-brag, but Chesterton sees this as a sign of saintly silliness, which the bishop recognized and so happily played along. Francis wasn't so much trying to shame his father as to point out the absurdity of his anxiety and remind everyone of exactly how absurd the Christian life can seem.

Francis' humor was self-deprecating. He called his body "Brother Ass" because it was stubborn as a mule, and after he received the holy *stigmata*—the wounds of Christ in his hands and feet and side—he would complain that while giving him extra holes that the Lord had neglected to take care of the ones that already existed in his head. But Francis' humor *always* had a point.

While staying in Rome trying to get his Order approved, Francis stayed with a certain cardinal. One night he was attacked by demons in the night and beaten pretty badly. When the cardinal questioned him about it in the morning, he smiled wryly and said that he presumed he'd been beaten by devils as punishment for hanging out with Cardinals. More famously, when he traveled to visit the Sultan of Egypt to try to convert him, the sultan laid a trap for him. He had a carpet brought in that had crosses embroidered on it. His plan was that if Francis walked on the carpet, he'd accuse him of insulting Christ. But if he refused to walk on the carpet, he'd act offended. Francis walked right onto the carpet, and when the sultan accused him of blasphemy, Francis responded, "Well, our Lord died between two thieves. We have the True Cross, but if you like having the thieves', then I won't blame you for it, but I'll walk on it just the same." He wasn't just funny, he was *witty*; his humor was purposeful and left an impression. His humor was what most impressed the sultan.

St. Francis was not the only religious founder to use humor with his followers. St. Dominic, St. Francis' contemporary who founded the Dominican Order, even told a joke in the midst of a miracle. Dominic had been away preaching and had just gotten a very important priest to agree to enter his new Order, but it had taken a lot of time. One late night, he reached a convent of the nuns he had founded, after the sisters had gone to bed. Most of the time he would have come in and gone to bed himself, but instead he instructed the superior to wake the sisters and call them to the dining room. There he told them about his success and, in the course of talking, asked for a cup of wine. One of the brothers who was there brought the wine and a cup, and Dominic blessed it, took a long, healthy drink himself, and then passed the cup on to the brothers. Several brothers were present, and though each drank his fill, the cup never ran dry. The sisters apparently noticed this, so he asked for a second cup and then did the same for them, saying as he passed the cup along, "Drink up, Daughters. The grace of God is plenty!"

St. Ignatius of Loyola, who founded the Jesuits, was also

famous for his wit and wisdom. He was, early on, called before the Inquisition for teaching "novelties" or new things. He responded that he didn't think it was an especially new thing to speak about Christ to Christians. That reply silenced the Inquisitors, and he was set free. He also frequently told his novices, "Laugh long and grow strong." For Ignatius, laughter was essential to a healthy spiritual life.

It's important that characters like Francis and Dominic and Ignatius were such advocates of laughter. Other voices in the Church at the time, always a minority but sometimes a vocal one, were afraid of humor. They thought that laughter contorted the face, or that it aroused the passions and broke down the will, like alcohol or drugs. The fact that hardly anyone remembers their names is testimony enough to the constant support of good humor in the Christian tradition and the hallmark of spiritual health.

Of course, neither Francis nor Dominic nor Ignatius invented this idea. They were simply staying faithful to the tradition which they themselves had received. The Fathers and Mothers of the Desert frequently used humor both to instruct their disciples but also to laugh at their own foibles. For example, a young man wanted to enter a monastery, but the abbot told him that he needed to grow in humility first. So the young man, wanting to prove that he was serious, started paying people to insult him; the worse the insult, the more he'd pay, so that over time this guy became famous for paying people to make fun of him. Eventually, he ran out of money and so returned to the monastery. The doorkeeper made fun of him as soon as he entered, and the young man started laughing. When the abbot came to see about the commotion, the young man explained, "For three years I've been paying people to do this for me, and I've spent a fortune doing it. I come here, and you do it for free."

The abbot smiled. Now the young man was ready to begin.

There's another good one about St. Moses the African, who had been a notorious outlaw—kind of the Jesse James of fourth-century Egypt—before he entered the monastery. One night a group of thieves broke into the monastery and were going to steal the altar vessels and such, but Moses stopped them, tied them up, and left them in front of the altar. When the monks arrived for prayers the next morning, the two prisoners were still there with Moses guarding them. When the abbot asked him what had happened, he replied, "In my former life, I would just have killed them, but I figured that's against the rules now. I just didn't know what to do with them instead."

Two old monks were once arguing over a brick and what it should be used for in the monastery, and the abbot wasn't around to mediate the dispute. So they decided to have a fist-fight to settle the matter, but they wound up in hysterics. They'd both been in the monastery for so long, they'd forgotten how to have a proper fight.

Even St. Jerome, who showed so little humor when dealing with St. Augustine, was willing to share a chuckle with his friends. He once wrote to a friend who had married into a pagan family devoted especially to the pagan god Jupiter. His comment, "I am sure that Jupiter himself would have become a Christian, if only he'd had a family as persistent as yours," was meant both to ease her anxiety over whether her family would ever convert, as well as show how silly her anxiety itself was— and especially the way she was allowing it to run her life.

There's probably no more stereotypically Catholic image than that of the serious-faced, angry-looking nun. Of course, in real life this is far from the truth. Most sisters are very happy, and there's a treasure trove of examples from the lives of the saints to show just how important humor can be in the convent.

St. Teresa of Avila, who was one of the greatest women to ever live and a Doctor of the Church, was also apparently hysterical. "From silly devotions and sour-faced saints, good Lord deliver us" was a frequent prayer of hers. When one of her nuns would write, always in Latin and always showing off her knowledge with quotations and long, difficult-to-read sentences, Teresa would reply, "God keep you from being a Latinist!" She even has a great joke right at the start of the *Interior Castle*, her greatest work and one of the most important books of theology every written. "So many books have been written by learned and holy men that it looks like there's nothing left for a woman to write about!"

Therese of Lisieux, the Little Flower of the twentieth century, was also a great one for jokes, pranks, and nicknames. Some of the photos which still exist of her show her dressed up as Joan of Arc for a play, but apparently she would periodically put on the costume, or at least part of it, and entertain the sisters at recreation. She had pet names for all of the sisters and frequently invented new ones for herself, always to poke fun at some particular foible. Even as she got sick with tuberculosis, she would tease the people who came to see her in the infirmary. Apparently, she would do things like tie the sister's rosaries in knots with her toes while they sat talking to her on the bed. Once, near the end, a priest came to anoint her but refused because she sat up in bed in order to be ready. She told the sister-in-charge, "Well, I'll just have to make more of an effort to look sick next time!" And the Little Flower may be the only saint on record to have made a joke from the grave. After she died, they laid her out next to the grill in the parlor of the convent so that people could come and view the body through the screen. The custom was, if the sister were especially holy, that laypeople would bring rosaries or medals to pass through the grill and that one of the sisters would then touch the object to the body before handing it back. Well, the young sister who was on duty was especially broken up about Sister Therese's death, and so at one point when someone handed her a rosary, it got tangled up in the corpse's hands. She worked and worked but couldn't get the chain free, which only made her cry more as the crowd on the other side of the grill was starting to grow anxious. Finally, she heard a voice interiorly that she knew to be Sister Therese's.

"I'm not going to let go until you give me a smile." The sister apparently responded silently, "No, I feel like crying," until she realized that she was arguing with a dead woman and then burst out laughing. Therese got her way, even in death.

One of the things which won the Church so many converts during the early days of persecution was their courage even in face of death. The Romans had a kind of stoic ideal about approaching death in a measured, almost emotionless way. The Christians one-upped them; not only were our martyrs not afraid of death, they often went to the lions or the sword or the gridiron laughing, singing, and in the sort of humor you might expect at a party, certainly not a funeral.

One of the most famous stories from this period is about St. Lawrence. He was a deacon in Rome in the middle 200s. The emperor had issued an edict calling for the death of all bishops, priests, and deacons. They caught Pope Sixtus saying Mass in the catacombs and beheaded him and six of his deacons. Lawrence, the seventh, was given three days to gather up "the treasures of the Church" to be turned over to the emperor. Instead he took those three days and distributed all of the Church's property among the members, especially the poor. Then, on the third day, Lawrence showed up with the poor, the crippled, and the destitute of the community. "These," he said, "are the treasures of the Church." The Romans thought that he was being smart, so instead of beheading him, as they had the others, they decided to roast him on a gridiron over a fire. He was making wise cracks right up to the end. After he'd been roasting for some time, he famously told his executioners, "I'm well done on this side. Flip me over now!"

Lawrence was only one of the first of many in a tradition that continues to this day. Probably the most famous and the funniest was St. Thomas More. During his legal and political career in England, More was known for his wit and humor, often joking with both plaintiffs and defendants in court and frequently satirizing guests at dinner parties. This made him very popular with the king, who also had a good sense of humor, but who also wanted a divorce.

When the king then declared himself head of the Church in England, More refused to submit to him. He was kept in prison for a year before being executed. On his way up the stairs to the chopping block he tipped the executioner saying, "I might need a hand up, but as for getting down, I think I'll manage on my own." Then after first setting his neck down to have his head cut off, he asked for a moment to adjust himself. His beard had grown quite long in prison, so he adjusted it so that it was sitting outside the block. "This," he said, tugging at his beard, "has not offended the king."

Sometimes God even seems to have a sense of humor when it comes to martyrdom. When the priests in Geneva were all rounded up by Protestant extremists to be executed, there was a really, really bad priest among them. This guy was a gambler who had embezzled lots of money from the Church, and a womanizer who had fathered a bunch of kids by different women. He was suspended and living in public shame, but when he was gathered up and asked to deny the Real Presence and the Pope, his response was, "Fornicator I always was; a heretic I never shall be." The ironic thing was that another priest was there that day, a very pious guy who had always seemed very devout. He was afraid of dying, so he did renounce the Blessed Sacrament and the pope; he lived and became a Protestant. But he always lived with the memory of that bad priest who had done better than he had and eventually he returned to the Faith and died a martyr too. God's writing straight with crooked lines isn't just clever; sometimes it's really funny too.

Now it would be easy reading all of this history to imagine that maybe saints had a good sense of humor once upon a time, but that nowadays Christians are serious folk. And certainly looking around your parish, it might seem like that. But don't worry, plenty of contemporary examples of saintly humor show us just how to use it as a weapon to grow in humility and get over ourselves.

G. K. Chesterton, who this chapter started with, was one of the funniest writers of the twentieth century. He was also one of the most devout Catholics in England. "Humor," he used to say, "can get in under the door while seriousness is still fumbling at the handle." He lived it too. Chesterton was a great big man—well over six feet tall and topping the scales around three hundred pounds. Even before he became obese, he had some health problems which prevented him from serving in the military. Once, during World War I, a woman approached him on the street and said, "Young man, why aren't you out at the front?" She was talking about "the front" of the war and was accusing Chesterton of draft dodging.

He replied with a smile, "Madam, if you'd come around the other side, I think you'd see that I am." Now I don't know about you, but if a stranger walked up to me on the street and insulted me I don't think I'd reply by poking fun at myself. But that's because I still have a long way to go in getting over myself. Chesterton, apparently, was well on his way.

Another holy man, St. John XXIII, was pope from 1958-1963. He'd been a papal diplomat before becoming pope and was thought to have averted more than one military conflict with just the right kind of joke at dinner. As pope he was famously asked, "How many people work in the Vatican?"

Without skipping a beat, he replied, "About half." When an American asked about the practice of the Italian siesta—the break in the afternoon so that people can take a nap—he said, "Your holiness, I understand that the Vatican is closed in the afternoon, and nobody works then."

He smiled and said, "No, the offices are closed in the afternoon. People don't work in the morning!"

And lest we think that holy men have the monopoly on humor these days, even St. Teresa of Calcutta was known to pull a prank or tell a joke. Once when visiting her sisters in Rome, she saw that a couple of seminarians were praying in her Order's chapel. Walking into the chapel, she approached a young man who looked the most senior and important. She stood up straight and looked right into his eye as though about to say something profound. "I have something to tell you," she whispered. He leaned forward, excited to receive a word from a living saint. "You're in my seat!"

St. John Paul II had a very playful personality and loved hats. Literally just do an image search for "John Paul II hats" and you'll get a slew of pictures, most of him either wearing a silly hat that he received as a gift or putting his white skullcap on somebody else. When the St. Louis Blues Hockey Team presented the aged pope with a hockey stick, he flipped the stick over and started dancing with it like a cane. Once as his health began to fail, he fell on the carpet at the Vatican and apparently did a perfect impression of the Italian version of the Medical Alert "I've-Fallen-And-I-Can't-Get-Up" lady. Of course, he was an actor before he became a priest.

The point is that the saints frequently use humor, but they use it differently than many of us tend to. Sitcoms weren't just the background noise to their lives, and stand-ups making fun of other people weren't a kind of escape from reality for them either. For the saints, both of yesterday and today, humor is an essential exercise in authentic humility.

Humility gets a bad rep, especially in an individualistic culture that prides itself on personal accomplishments. But true, authentic humility can never be about diminishing one's gifts

or talents, ingratitude for what God has given, or a lack of charity—either toward one's self or somebody else. True humility is
self-knowledge in action. A humble basketball player doesn't
pretend that she's bad at her sport; she acknowledges her gifts,
gives thanks for having had the chance to develop her skills,
and works to pass on her knowledge to other people. She stays
open to learning and growing and developing but refuses to
hide the gift she has been given. Likewise, a talented musician
doesn't play down his talent, refuse to play for other people
or to teach those just learning. The humble musician plays;
he plays for fun; he plays for practice; he plays for Church; he
plays for work; he plays for love and for fear, for frustration and
delight; but he plays, and he plays *because God has given him
the grace to play.*

"Pride goeth before the fall" is actually a slight misquota-
tion; the original is from the book of Proverbs and says, *"Pride
goes before disaster, and a haughty spirit before a fall"* (Proverbs
16:18). We all know what it's like to get too cocky, to presume
we know something only to learn that we don't, or to pitch
an argument too forcefully only to be proven wrong. But the
scriptures aren't so much worried about our making fools of
ourselves and getting embarrassed. Instead, this functions as
a warning against that overall attitude of entitlement, against a
presumption in our favor over and against everybody else, and
reminds us again and again and again that *everything we have
is a gift.*

Everyone is called to humility, and when we really think

about it, most of the people we admire best, in whatever field, are those we perceive as genuinely humble. The contrary is also true; people are attracted to confidence, but not to outright arrogance. That's the meaning of Mary's prophecy in the *Magnificat*: *"He has cast down the mighty from their thrones, but lifted up the lowly."*

So the art of getting over yourself depends entirely upon your ability to cultivate the skill of humility, and learning to laugh at yourself and with others is the best place to start. You've got to become more humble in order to get better, to get over yourself to get into the lives of other people, and to focus on gratitude in order to avoid entitlement. We have great models who have gone ahead of us, powerful advocates who work on our behalf even now, and strong remedies in the sacraments, especially Confession and Holy Communion. For just as God shows Himself humble—humble enough to embrace our humanity, humble enough to become our very Food and Drink—so we too have the chance to live a life of true humility: the opportunity, the grace, to share even now in the life of God Himself.

QUESTIONS FOR REFLECTION

Do I laugh often enough? Do I take myself too seriously?

How can I grow in humility just a little every day? How can I use humor as a tool in my spiritual life?

CHAPTER TEN

MARY'S MANTLE

Dear Mother of God, I find that I am more fortunate than you. For I have you as a mother.

— St. Therese of Lisieux

ONE OF MY favorite memories from growing up was at a Fourth-of-July parade when I was about five or six. My mom and I were crowded with the rest of the families next to the curb so that we could see the floats and catch the candy. Something came by—a tractor, a classic car, a float somebody made in a high school gym, and the candy started to fly. This great big piece landed right on the ground in front of me, but as I bent to pick it up, another mom came barreling in from the right. She pushed past a couple of people and literally *stepped* over me to get to the candy on the ground. She probably would've knocked me right down if it hadn't been for my mom. Fortunately, she saw the lady coming before I did. Leaning forward, she reached out and pulled me back right before the lady ran into me. Mom didn't punch her or anything, though I'm sure she wanted to; in fact, I don't even remember her saying anything to her. But a look passed between them that said everything which needed to be said, and we didn't see that woman or her kid the rest of the parade.

My mother taught me what motherhood means that day. I already knew about good-night kisses and favorite foods, about toys and books and time spent cuddling. I even knew about getting scolded when I did something wrong or being stopped when I could hurt myself. What I did not know until that day was that motherhood was about more than just *defending* your kid; it's about taking the *offensive* when it comes to his or her welfare. Mothering is like labor; it can *look* passive because you're on your back or scrunched up in a ball, but it's about the most *active* thing you can really do.

To be honest, a part of me feels like I shouldn't be the one writing this chapter; I feel like my wife or my mom should be. But my wife says I have to, and my mom always tells me to listen to my wife, and they're both usually right! The thing is, you don't have *to be a mother* to understand what it is to *have a mother,* and that's the whole point of Mary for us. Whatever our relationship with the woman who gave birth to us, *we all have a mother,* and she's a lot rougher, tougher, and active than we usually give her credit for.

One of the oldest hymns to Mary is sung on the feast of the Annunciation and the Sundays leading up to it in the Byzantine Churches. It goes like this:

> To thee, the Champion Leader,
> we thy servants dedicate

a feast of victory and of thanksgiving
as ones rescued out of sufferings,
O Theotokos: but as thou art one
with might which is invincible,
from all dangers that can be
do thou deliver us,
that we may cry to thee:
Rejoice, O Bride Unwedded!

I've only recently discovered this song, but I love it—mostly because it turns a lot of the images that we have about our Blessed Mother upside down. The song helps remind us of how powerful some of those images are—things we've just gotten used to.

A lot of us picture Mary as this meek and mild creature, as though she spent her whole life sitting in a corner with her hands folded on her lap, looking holy. But that's very different than the story scripture gives. In fact, the first thing we see Mary doing is making decisions—decisions that will have an impact not only on the rest of her life, but on the rest of our lives too.

Mary said, *"Behold, I am the handmaid of the Lord. May it be done to me according to your word." Then the angel departed from her"* (Luke 1:38).

We often imagine the Annunciation as this very passive event: Mary sitting at home, praying or doing some light work around the house, the angel's visiting, and her muttering a very quiet, "Well all right, whatever you think is best" to the angel.

But that's not how the Bible tells the story. Instead, the angel first freaks her out and then tries to calm her down by telling her that something impossible is about to happen, which seems to make her freak out more. She, understandably, does not understand, and the angel doesn't scold her but makes a further prophecy and offers proof of what he says about Mary's relative, who like her is mysteriously and impossibly pregnant. Only then does Mary give her consent, but it's about as far away from a passive "All right" as you can imagine. Even the imagery Mary uses, that is, what we've passed down through the generations and usually misunderstood, is *proactive*. Mary is a handmaid, not in the sense that she's weak or unimportant, but in the sense that she would have known, like the handmaidens from the Psalms.

> *Yes, like the eyes of servants on the hand of their masters, like the eyes of a maid on the hand of her mistress, So our eyes are on the* LORD *our God, till we are shown favor* (Psalm 123:3).

Mary consents to God's will, but *actively*—not passively. She's eager to please her Master, and she waits anxiously, as her people have for generations, for God to show His mercy.

From that moment onward, Mary's life is lived as an *agent* of God's will. The very first thing she does is travel to visit her relative whom the angel had mentioned. Again, sometimes we domesticate this story. Of course Mary was anxious to share the news about her pregnancy, and of course, relatives come in to help when it's time to have a baby, *but these were no ordinary babies*, and they were two *very extraordinary* mothers. In the Visitation to her cousin, Elizabeth, Mary shows us what getting over yourself looks like in real life: it means putting your money where your mouth is and getting to work on behalf of those who need you.

That's the reason why the hymn uses military imagery to talk about the Blessed Mother. She is the *Champion Leader*, literally the general in God's army. There are even icons of Mary in full chain mail and armor—not because anybody thinks she ever served in a military—but because she's a kind of spiritual warrior. During her life on earth, she was meek and mild and sweet and loving, but she was also tough and feisty and ambitious for the Kingdom. What many fail to realize, though, is that her work did not end in death, but continues today—even as she continues to guide and protect and direct the work of her children, the members of the Church.

The problem with our images of the Blessed Mother isn't that we've made her *too maternal,* but that we have mixed-up and overly sentimental ideas about *just what motherhood is.* Nothing was passive about Mary's participation in God's plan, just as there's nothing passive about any woman going through pregnancy, labor, and delivery.

I was there when my kids were born, and while my wife may have been on the bed, she was doing more work there than I have ever done. And as she and I have grown together as parents, it's more and more clear to me that there's nothing passive or weak or soft about nursing and changing and bathing and playing and feeding and caring and protecting and advocating for your kids.

We Catholics say the *Hail Mary* so often that, most of the time, the words fall out of our mouths without our even thinking of them. Our Eastern cousins, who wrote the hymn I quoted earlier in this chapter, pay a little better attention to them. "Holy Mary, Mother of God..." We pray, *Theotokos*; they say, *the God-bearer*.

That little word, which we take so for granted, caused one of the greatest controversies in the history of the Church. There were riots in the fourth century, and people were exiled and killed, all over calling Mary the Mother of God. Because if Mary is the mother of Jesus, and Jesus is God as we say, then she *must* be the *Mother of God*. And that makes everything different.

You see, it's only *because* Mary is the Mother of God that we stand a real chance of finally getting over ourselves. On our own, we can work ourselves to the bone—building new habits and getting rid of old ones, letting go of grudges and building new and holy friendships, praying, receiving the sacraments, and doing good works. However, in the end, we're not going to get very far—not all on our own. We need grace; we need grace like a fish needs water, and Mary is both the sign and the promise that if we're open to receiving grace and actively engaging our God, then the grace will come through when we most need it.

Mary may have been *the* Mother of God, the *Theotokos*, but we are all called to be *Theotokoi*, the *bearers of God* to the world. Mary's place in the story will always be unique, and because she did it first she will also be responsible for helping us accomplish our part, but our vocations are not so distinct. Mary listened to God's word for years, prepared herself and was prepared by God in contemplation; only then was the time right for her to *conceive* God in her heart, her soul, and her very body. And only after coming to know the Presence of God inside her, to sit with it and let it gestate, to get to know its movements from the inside out, only then was she able *to bear* it, to give birth to God in the world. Mary's birth pangs didn't end at Bethlehem, they followed her everywhere she followed Him—to the cross and beyond. And we, like her, will struggle and suffer as we work to bear God's presence to the world as well.

Every year, especially at Christmas time, but sometimes at Easter too, some people (the ones I don't invite to my dinner parties) freak out about the various cultural depictions of the Holy Family. The usual worry is that the characters are all too white; after all, Mary and Joseph and Jesus and pretty much the whole cast of biblical characters were Middle-Eastern Jews. And it's certainly true that most European and American nativity scenes feature characters that look, well, American or European. But that criticism presumes that the point of the artwork is photorealistic—as though the idea was simply to imagine what the "real" Nativity of Jesus actually looked like and represent that as best we can. Of course, that's not usually the point of religious art at all.

If we look deeper, every culture that has accepted the Christian Faith has found a way to make Jesus and Mary their own. There are African Marys and Jesuses, Indian, East Asian, West Asian, Polynesian, Native American, Australian Aboriginal; I've even seen an Inuit Madonna and Child complete with a baby Jesus wrapped in a sealskin coat. Jesus, Mary, and Joseph, and all the events of our salvation really did happen in a real time and a real place, but their effects are seen and felt and lived out by us for the rest of history. Our art is meant to reflect that reality, not first-century fashion.

Of course, our lives are too, and here most of us struggle even more than with the art because learning the "art" of getting over yourself is not so different than learning the "art" of painting or sculpture or screen-printing. Learning an art requires skill, which takes time to develop, dedication and discipline, the help of others more experienced, and the support of those who believe in your project. In short, it requires the Church to lead and guide, to shape and form, and to support and challenge as you grow.

When it comes to Mary we, her children, tend to make one of two mistakes, and they are terribly similar to the mistakes we make when it comes to our own mothers. Our first instinct is to divinize her and to make her more than she is because of who she has been for all of us. The problem with this is that it removes her from our experience, it makes her too distant, and it becomes easy to dismiss her example because she was *so* special, or graced, or chosen in a way that we have not been. It makes living up to her ideals an unrealistic waste of time. This is a mistake I know that I too often fall into myself.

The second mistake is to make her too familiar. In this way, Mary's experience is no different than our own at all, and therefore, she has nothing really to teach us, nothing to offer. This line of thinking makes her at best into any other saint, and at worst, into any other person. This is the mistake that those who are uncomfortable with traditional devotion to Mary—either Catholic or Protestant—tend to make.

But the truth is, somewhere in between, or perhaps better, holding both to be true at the same time. Mary is *both* special and normal, chosen and ordinary, waiting on the Lord and anxious to do His will. And you know what? *So are we!*

The popes often end their documents and the letters they write to the Church with a few words on Mary. I thought I'd do the same—not because I think I'm pope (God help the Church!), but because they're right to do so. Mary is the one who not only reminds us of what we can be, but she shows us how to get there. And because she already enjoys the life that we're aiming for, she can help us along the way as well. She is, in that way, both *with* and *for* us.

When Mary finally did make it to Elizabeth's house, she sang a song. The song was old, inspired by the song which Hannah sang when she became pregnant with the prophet Samuel, another woman who wasn't supposed to get pregnant who wound up having a baby who would change the world. The Church came to call Mary's song *the Magnificat* because those are the first words of the song in Latin. In English, it goes like this:

My soul proclaims the greatness of the Lord;
my spirit rejoices in God my savior.
For he has looked upon his handmaid's lowliness;
behold, from now on will all ages call me blessed.
The Mighty One has done great things for me,
and holy is his name.
His mercy is from age to age
to those who fear him.
He has shown might with his arm,
dispersed the arrogant of mind and heart.
He has thrown down the rulers from their thrones
but lifted up the lowly.
The hungry he has filled with good things;
the rich he has sent away empty.
He has helped Israel his servant,
remembering his mercy,
according to his promise to our fathers,
to Abraham and to his descendants forever
(Luke 1:46-55).

This is the song of someone who has gotten over themselves. *This* is what a life lived for God and others really looks like. *This* is everything I've ever said summed up in just a few lines.

Now it's true that Mary had special graces—graces given her from the first moment of her conception—which protected her from sin and its effects and better enabled her to respond to the work of God in her life. But she was given those graces precisely *so that we could see* what it is we're supposed to look like. She bore Christ in the flesh so that we could bear Him in the Spirit; she lived a life for others so that we could learn how to get over ourselves. She lived—and lives—*with and for* us, so that we could learn to get over ourselves and live for others too.

Mary never had to "get over herself" in the same way that we do, but she certainly had a lot to get over in her life: poverty, humiliation, and oppression to name a few. But in the end, she shows us how God works in the lives of those who trust Him, shows us that His mercy runs through all generations, that He scatters the proud and powerful and lifts up the weak and lowly, and that He always, always stays faithful to His promises.

God has made promises to each of us. Just as He made a covenant with Abraham and with Moses on Mount Sinai long ago, just as He vowed again and again through the mouths of His prophets, and just as He sealed His love in the blood of His Only-Begotten Son, so too He has made a promise **to you**. At your baptism, He adopted you; He guaranteed all of the graces necessary not only for you to reach heaven later, but to be the best you can be here and now. He swore to help you get over yourself and get on to living for others, to living for Him—and He will not go back on His word.

The Dominicans tell a story about St. Dominic. When he was first founding his Order, a whole lot of people, including the pope, didn't think it was going to last. Well, one night he had a dream or a vision. He was brought up to heaven, and he saw huge crowds of monks and nuns thronging around the throne of God. They were from every different religious order in the Church and many he'd never seen before. But he saw none of his own; no one was wearing his order's habit, and he could not spot any of his brothers or sisters in the crowd. He began to cry and asked, "Where are *my* brothers and sisters?"

Our Lord approached him and said, "Would you like to see your brothers?"

And when Dominic nodded his head, our Lady pulled back her mantle—her cloak—and sheltered there underneath her cape were more Dominicans than poor Dominic could count.

The Dominicans love telling that story for obvious reasons, but the same can be true for all of us, and you don't have to become a Dominican to wind up under our Lady's mantle. All you have to do is recognize her role—in God's life, in the life of the Church, and in your own life.

Where are you going to find a better model? Who is going to teach you better how to love the way you should? Who is going to show you a more effective way to getting over yourself? And who is going to offer you more and better protection—from your past and your grudges, from your vices and bad habits, from relationships that hold you back, and bad ideas that keep you from succeeding? Who else is going to care enough to keep you under her cape? And where are you going to find a better place to be?

As you prepare to step out now and put some of these ideas into practice, put yourself under our Lady's protection and know that I am offering prayers on your behalf as well. I pray each day for those who read my books and hear my talks. And if you're open to it, more graces than you can count are available to you. Then, when you see the Lord, you'll have no reason to weep. Instead, with Mary, you'll find yourself rejoicing because God will have lifted you up out of your old self and helped to shape you into a new person—the one you were always meant to be. Then you will truly be a man or woman of God and a man or woman for others.

QUESTIONS FOR REFLECTION

How can I cultivate a closer relationship with Mary? Do I pray to her often or seldom? What are my favorite images of her?

CONCLUSION

I CAN'T MAKE you a saint, and no book or set of prayers or specialized diet or extreme exercise program can either. Even you can't make yourself a saint, though you don't stand a chance if you don't at least make yourself ready for the graces that God is longing to give you. But in the end, the goal of your life, of every life—to be a saint—is ultimately a work of God. Our job is to clear out the clutter of our lives and make space for God to act. Our job is to get over ourselves and get on to God. Let's get to work.

NOTES

ABOUT THE AUTHOR

J ON LEONETTI IS a nationally known Catholic speaker, best-selling author and radio host who conveys a message of lasting fulfillment in Jesus Christ. Through Jon's keynote presentations and parish missions, thousands of Catholics each year discover the freedom Christ offers by way of his life and love.

Jon's first two books—*Mission of the Family* and *Your God Is Too Boring*—are published and featured in Matthew Kelly's Dynamic Catholic book program. They have been endorsed by Archbishop Joseph E. Kurtz, New York Times Bestselling author Immaculee Ilibagiza, Dr. Peter Kreeft, Brandon Vogt, Tom Peterson and more.

Jon believes that our deepest longing for happiness and wholeness is fulfilled in the encounter with Jesus Christ. Through prayer, the Sacraments, family life, and the help of Mary and the saints, Jon wants to cultivate an intimate relationship with Jesus and help others do the same.

With this message Jon has been featured and interviewed by the nation's top Catholic websites, blogs and radio shows, helping Catholics in all walks of life to fall in love and stay in love with the living God.

At home, Jon enjoys reading, sports, exercising, coffee and, most of all, spending time with his wife Teresa and their children, Joseph and Gianna.

Learn more at www.JonLeonetti.com